LAVENDER REFLECTIONS

Affirmations for Lesbians & Gay Men

FRANCISCAN CENTER
1784 LaCrosse Avenue
St. Paul, MN 55119

Keep affirming yourself and others
Eleanor Ruth Wagner

LAVENDER REFLECTIONS

Affirmations for Lesbians & Gay Men

Eleanor Ruth Wagner

Photographs by Victor Arimondi

ALAMO SQUARE PRESS
San Francisco

Copyright © 1995 by Eleanor Ruth Wagner.

All rights reserved. Printed in the United States of America. No part of this book may be used or reproduced in any manner whatsoever without written permission except in the case of brief quotations embodied in critical articles or reviews. For information, address Alamo Square Press, P.O. Box 14543, San Francisco, CA 94114.

Grateful acknowledgment is made for permission to reprint the following: excerpts from *The Dyke Daily Companion*, by Mel White, Mackaw Press, © 1991, used by permission; excerpt from "Can Lesbians Be Friends?" by Margy, from *Lesbian Connection*, the free nationwide forum of news and ideas for, by and about lesbians. For info write LC c/o Ambitious Amazons, P.O. Box 811, East Lansing, MI 48826; poem XII ("The laws of God, the laws of man") from *Last Poems* from *The Collected Poems of A.E. Housman*, © 1922 by Henry Holt & Company, Inc., © 1950 by Barclays Bank Ltd., reprinted by permission of Henry Holt & Company, Inc.; excerpts from "The Politics of Silence," by Paul Monette, March 7, 1993 (op ed), © 1993 by The New York Times Company, reprinted by permission; excerpts quoting Yako Myers from "Caretakers of Earth" by Mike Steele, February 7, 1992, and quoting Erin in "Growing Up Gay" by Kurt Chandler, December 6, 1992, reprinted with permission of the *Star Tribune, Minneapolis-St. Paul*; lyrics from the song, "It Won't Take Long" from the audio recording, *Shadows on a Dime* by Ferron, 1984, Nemesis Publishing, used by permission; lyrics from the song, "Didn't Want to Say Goodbye" from the audio recording *Dance in the Moment*, by Judy Fjell, © 1985 Judy Fjell (BMI), used by permission; excerpt from video "Women Like Us," © Suzanne Neild and Rosalind Pearson; lyric from song "We Will Rise" from the the audio recording *Self Portrait, 1993* by Joseph Victor Sieger; excerpt from the unpublished paper, "How Can Someone Be Both Christian and Homosexual?" by The Rev. Dan Geslin, used by permission; lyrics from the song, "Expedition Song" on the audio recording *Just Can't Stop*, words and music by Ann Reed, © 1986 Turtlecub Publishing, used by permission; excerpt of young lesbian from "Veronica 4 Rose, U.K. Channel 4 television documentary, 1983, directed by Melanie Chait, © Melanie Chait Productions, used by permission; lyrics from song "Frontier" on *Live Dream* audio recording and "Waterfall" on *The Changer and the Changed* audio recording by Cris Williamson, © Bird Ankles Music, 1971, 1977, 1975 (BMI), all rights reserved, used by permission; poem by Bert Herrman, in *Being • Being Happy • Being Gay*, used by permission; excerpts from *Lesbian Passion* by JoAnn Loulan, © 1987 JoAnn Loulan, used by permission; excerpt of Marty Rockland from video, *Who Happen to Be Gay* by Dale Beldin and Mark Krenzien, published by Direct Cinema Limited, P.O. Box 10003, Santa Monica, CA 90410, Phone 310-396-4774, © 1979 Dale Beldin and Mark Krenzien; excerpts of Elizabeth Birch and Marilyn Gum from video *Out in Suburbia*, © Pam Walton Productions 1988, used by permission; lyrics from song "Backing Off and Pulling Away" by Holly Near on audio recording *Watch Out*, © 1983 by Hereford Music, used with permission, Ms. Near's music available on Redwood Records, P.O. Box 10408, Oakland, CA 94610, 1-800-888-SONG; excerpt from untitled poem, April 1994 [unpublished], by Sue Schlangen, used by permission; excerpt from "Quilt Poem II", by Kayla Collins, published in *Search: A Mosaic from the Plymouth Writers Group*, used by permission; poems "Breakdown" and "Winter" and excerpt from "Moving On" published in *Journeys*, by Margareth Cecilia Miller, © 1994 by Margareth Cecilia Miller, used by permission; excerpt of Vito Russo from film "Common Threads—Stories from the Quilt" directed by Rob Epstein and Jeffrey Friedman, © 1989 Telling Pictures, Inc. and The NAMES Project Foundation, courtesy The Filmmakers; journal entry by Ann E. Bancroft, written during the American Women's Trans-Antarctic Expedition, 1992-1993 [unpublished], used by permission; excerpts from Deb Price columns, 1993, GNS Features, reprinted with permission of *The Detroit News*; lyric from "It's Up to Me and You" by Tret Fure on *Terminal Hold* audio recording, © 1980 Lunafish Music, used by permission; the lines from Poem XIII of "Twenty-One Love Poems" are reprinted from *The Fact of a Doorframe, Poems Selected and New, 1950-1984*, by permission of the author and W. W. Norton & Company, Inc. © 1984 by Adrienne Rich. © 1975, 1978 by W. W. Norton & Company, Inc. © 1981 by Adrienne Rich.

Library of Congress Number: 95-079172

ISBN: 1-886360-02-2

10 9 8 7 6 5 4 3 2 1

To Kathy
Whose love has helped me
to be more than I could have been alone

Acknowledgements

When I first conceived the idea for this book, there were no others on the market of its kind. In the years it has taken for my idea to become reality, other books have come out, but I continued in my efforts, believing that I had something unique to offer. Many people have given me support along the way, and I am very grateful.

I want to thank several people in particular. Kayla Collins gave me gentle but honest feedback, supported me in my integrity and continually reminded me of the importance of my work. Margareth Miller helped me stay in touch with the joy of writing and shared the beauty of her person and poetry. Sue Schlangen offered wise insights and willingly shared her deeply personal self with me and my readers. Jan Logelin did the word-processing of the permissions letters and even *enjoyed* it! Arlene and Pat from the writers' group suggested many creative title ideas, one of which was *Lavender Reflections*. Kathy Hayden, my partner, encouraged me to follow my dreams, even when it challenged our relationship, and cleaned the house many times to give me more time to work on my writing.

I am grateful to Bert Herrman, my publisher, for following the spirit voice that told him to publish this book. All of us in the lesbian and gay community have benefitted in many ways from his dedication to providing high quality publications for us. I appreciate the diligent work of Arthur Evans in editing my book, with his careful attention to detail and unfailing commitment to excellence.

The Out-to-Brunch writers' group provided an always enthusiastic audience to my reading, with valuable critiquing and encouragement to stay true to my vision. The volunteers at Quatrefoil Library in St. Paul have developed a wonderful facility with extensive lesbian and gay resources as well as a friendly and accepting atmosphere in which to work. The Sunday afternoon Gay and Lesbian Adult Children of Alcoholics group introduced me to affirmations and inspired this book.

Introduction

All of us deserve to treasure ourselves. In a culture that provides too little affirmation, especially to those of us who are lesbian and gay, we need constant reminders of how beautiful we are and how natural our loving is. My longing for a written collection of such writings, consistent with the lesbian me, has birthed this book.

When I started using affirmations, my fragile self-esteem made it difficult to give myself positive messages. I chose to use what fit, and ignore the rest. Surprisingly, after a while I was comfortably giving myself affirmations that earlier had felt untrue. This has been a powerful process in my life. I encourage you to be gentle with yourself and find a way of using this book that feels right for you. If something does not seem to apply, leave it alone, or find your own words to make it work for where you are today.

All of us need to develop an independent sense of self-worth that will endure in the absence of external approval, but some external support is essential It is my hope that this book will help you build that strong inner belief in your value and also serve as validation from outside yourself, especially with respect to the goodness of your same-sex loving. The underlined affirmations in this book are phrased for you to say to yourself in your process of loving the special person you are. The accompanying meditations are worded to help you personalize the messages for your life.

Each entry relates to some aspect of our same-sex orientation and how it fits into our lives as a whole. Special emphasis is given to holidays, since those days are often stressful for lesbians and gay men. The first offering is a birthday affirmation, the holiday that can be the most affirming of all. For non-holidays, I have written an affirmation and meditation for every other day rather than daily, with the thought that our same-sex orientation is not the totality of who we are. I encourage you to use a more general affirmation or meditation source on alternate days. For those dates, I have included a quotation as a thought for the day or a suggestion for your personal reflection with space to write your ideas. All quotations are from people believed to be lesbian, gay or bisexual—a sample of the inspiring sources within our community.

Although I found it particularly difficult to write in terms that would resonate for both lesbians and gay men, my commitment to finding commonality between us led me to persist. Each of us is a beautiful and lovable person. May we grow in love for ourselves and appreciation of our radiance.

-Eleanor Ruth Wagner

Birthday

Self-Celebration

I exist as I am, that is enough.
If no other in the world is aware I sit content,
And if each and all be aware I sit content.

Walt Whitman
Song of Myself

<u>On my birthday, I celebrate the wonder of me.</u>

My birthday is the perfect time to affirm myself. I am ready to move beyond negative thoughts, such as getting old, falling short of my goals or not getting what I want. Today I focus on the positive: my valuable experience, real accomplishments and vision for the future.

I brightened the world the day I was born, and I continue to offer it true gifts. Every aspect of my being is beautiful, including my same-sex loving. When I am tempted to label myself as "different," I claim my uniqueness. I let myself feel good about all that I am and how my presence on this earth is important. I enjoy recognition from others, but I celebrate myself today.

I deserve to have a happy birthday. Today is not a time to be humble. This is my own holiday, and I am the star of it!

January

January 1
New Year's Day

Individualism

I name the parts of me I *don't* want to change, the parts of me that are fine just the way they are _____
_____
_____

<u>I set my own timetable of growth.</u>

My inner voice lets me know when I am ready for growth. Change is vital to my aliveness, but I resist change when it threatens the core of who I am. I deny the robot the controlling world would choose for me to be, and listen to myself.

On this holiday, special emphasis is placed on "self-improvement." When others pressure me to make new year's resolutions in their image, especially when that pressure relates to my sexual orientation, I listen to my inner guidance. I am getting better all the time, but my growth is stimulated from within, according to the plan that is right for me.

I give myself permission to be who I am today, not to change a bit, if that is my heart's desire. My beginnings happen as I am ready, not according to the calendar. The new me is the person being born from my inner light.

January 2   **Coming Out**

My Coming Out Day was the day I discovered a "secret" about myself. It seemed that no one really wanted me to know that secret, but thank the powers that be, I found out anyway.

And now that I know, there's no reason to keep it a secret anymore.

Mel White
The Dyke Daily Companion

January 3   **Coming Out**

I rejoice that I am discovering who I am.

I think back to my first awareness of my same-sex orientation. Coming out to myself, admitting my true sexual orientation, was the beginning of a lifelong process. I remember signs along the way, times when I may have tried to hide from myself. I also remember finally being willing to accept the truth of who I am.

So many emotions vying with each other—pain at being different, peace in finding an answer in my life, fear of the inevitable oppression, excitement in anticipating my natural loving, anger at the difficulty of the road before me, satisfaction in the sense of congruency within myself.

I knew my life wouldn't get any easier, but it wasn't easy up to that point either. I have survived many difficult moments since that first one, and there will be difficult moments ahead of me, but my path is clear.

I rejoice in accepting who I am. Some people never find themselves. I have accomplished much in my life. I am honest with myself. I pronounce myself *good*!

January 4   **Friendship**

The friendships...made me aware that what I needed in my life was not more or different lovers, but simply good friends. Having good friends to talk and laugh with, to hold, and hug, and sleep with (when I say sleep, that's exactly what I mean) finally, made me realize what I'd been missing as a single [person].

Margy
Lesbian Connection

January 5 — Friendship

<u>I draw caring people into my life.</u>

I know I need people. If I have a lover who gives me support, I still need friends and acquaintances. I deserve to have caring friends, and I reach out to find them.

Isolation has been the path of least resistance in my life. As I've sensed my differentness from others, it has been easy to withdraw and spend time alone. Others may have sensed the difference and avoided me, or I may have set up a wall that kept them away. Once I was able to define myself in terms of my same-sex attractions, it became even more difficult to be open because of my fear of rejection. I feel self-conscious sometimes, even when I am surrounded by lesbians and gay men. The old patterns linger beyond their usefulness.

As I become healthier, I take down my walls to let others in. I open myself in spite of my fears and ask for what I want and need. If one person cannot respond as I desire, I turn to other people. I offer my friendship and invite new friends into my life.

January 6 — Lessons of Nature

I've never outraged Nature. I've always listened to her advice and followed it wherever it went.

Joe Orton
quoted by Leigh W. Rutledge
Unnatural Quotations

January 7 — Lessons of Nature

<u>The resilience of the flowers lives within me.</u>

Looking around me, I see life triumphing over difficulty. A lovely flower grows through a crack in the rocks. Its beauty is so delicate, but what strength it took to thrive in such harsh conditions! How could it find enough soil for its roots? How did it catch the scant drops of water trickling past? How has it withstood the strong winds?

Having suffered oppression over my sexual orientation, I identify with that little flower—striving to bloom in an unaccepting world. I struggle to find place for my roots. I thirst for the plentiful resources others seem to find easily. I brace myself against the hostile forces of a homophobic world.

Sensing my oneness with the flower, I perceive my own strength and beauty. As the flower flourishes, I know that I too can do more than merely survive. Tiny flowers blossom, and so do I!

January 8   **Self-Liberation**

The laws of God, the laws of man
He may keep that will and can
Not I: let God and man decree
Laws for themselves and not for me;
And if my ways are not as theirs
Let them mind their own affairs.
Their deeds I judge and much condemn,
Yet when did I make laws for them?

                                                                                 A.E. Housman
                                                                              "Last Poems, XII"
                                          The Collected Poems of A.E. Housman

January 9   **Self-Liberation**

<u>I am liberated by following love's higher law.</u>

    My own gay liberation starts with my personal resolve. I determine my path by deciding to live in love and choosing how best to do that in my life.

    As a child, I was taught about the importance of obeying the law. Those who broke laws were bad people and were put in jail. Although most sodomy laws apply to heterosexuals as well as homosexuals, the selective enforcement of sodomy laws with gay men dramatizes how I am looked upon by the "establishment" as a criminal because of my same-sex loving.

    This invasion of the government into my bedroom makes it difficult to be unashamed in my lovemaking. When I focus on the intimacy I experience with my loved one and block out all the negative messages bombarding me, I know the rightness of my loving. I obey a law much higher than those devised by homophobic legislators—my heart's commitment to what is most loving in my life. With pride, I live outside the law in the integrity of my caring.

January 10   **Beauty in Loving**

It is so true that a woman may be in love with a woman, and a man with a man. It is pleasant to be sure of it, because it is undoubtedly the same love that we shall feel when we are angels...

                                                                                Margaret Fuller
                                                          Woman in the Nineteenth Century

January 11 — Beauty in Loving

<u>In the beauty of others' bodies, I see my own.</u>

Beautiful people, beautiful bodies. I am one with my gender as I appreciate the loveliness of all of us.

My culture has worked hard to make me feel inferior for loving someone of my own gender. However, my sexual orientation is playing a wonderful joke on that oppressive culture. Every time I am attracted to someone of my same sex, I am seeing the beauty that is me. Every time I make love to a person with a body like mine, I am realizing what a wonderful body I have. Whenever I celebrate my same-sex loving, I am generating pride in myself as a lovable person.

The messages from the mainstream are strong, but I let the positive messages from myself overwhelm those negative ones. The greater my bonds with those of my same gender, the greater my love for myself. What a marvelous trick to play on the world!

January 12 — Commitment

I plan to stay with the person I'm with for years and years. I think to be gay is to be blessed. We have so much freedom, so many choices. This isn't our moment to party or to think we're going to stay young forever...maybe it's our time to find someone to be safe with...to be happy with.

Kurt Marshall
quoted by Leigh W. Routledge
Unnatural Quotations

January 13 — Commitment

<u>I build healthy, intimate relationships.</u>

Having a deep, enduring relationship is an option for me. If I dream of a long-term sexual relationship or am involved with someone and want to continue, I wish for some assurance of it being possible. I see so few people, either gay or straight, who seem happy together.

Loving someone of the same sex offers me many opportunities. I can have an equal relationship with my partner more easily than a man and woman raised with norms of male dominance. I can negotiate my commitment without pressure to follow traditional marriage vows. I have already rejected the heterosexist rules in my coming out process—I can ignore the relationship restrictions too.

It takes courage to be a pioneer, but is it really harder than being a slave to restrictive rules and stereotypes? Healthy role models might make it easier, but the truth is, intimacy by trial and error is the only way there is! Today I visualize a vibrant enduring love and know it is within me.

January 14   **Aspirations**

It now had been laid to my charge to keep my own heart free of hatred and despair.
James Baldwin
Notes of a Native Son

January 15   **Aspirations**
Martin Luther King Junior's Birthday

<u>I share the dream of an all-loving world.</u>
    Today I take hope from Martin Luther King, Jr.'s dream as I find my own vision to sustain me. Although his oppression was different from what I experience in my same-sex orientation, there is a commonality in what each of us has endured as a member of an oppressed group. Much needs to change before racism is gone from this planet, just as extensive progress is needed in the area of lesbian and gay rights. On this holiday, I celebrate the life of one who dared to believe in a better world and worked to make it happen. I appreciate how his work for African-American civil rights opened many eyes to injustices of all kinds and eased our fight for lesbian and gay rights.
    Reverend King's courage, perseverance, and commitment to nonviolence inspire me, and I strive for these qualities in my living. I too have a contribution to make in this world. I affirm the value of my mission, whether it is through my work, my relationships, or simply how I live. I aspire to the greatness of heart shown by all women and men who have worked for the betterment of humankind.

January 16   **Sexual Orientation**

Oh, you mean I'm homosexual! Of course I am, and heterosexual too. But what's that got to do with my headache?
Edna St. Vincent Millay
quoted by Leigh W. Rutledge
Unnatural Quotations

January 17   **Sexual Orientation**

<u>I alone define my sexual orientation.</u>
    I am the final authority on me, and I know my sexual attractions. Some people would like to assign everyone to one of three mutually exclusive categories: heterosexual, homosexual or bisexual. Acknowledging the complexities of human beings, though, I expand my view of sexuality to include a wide variety of sexual identies and attractions. Like a bird on a utility wire, I place myself along the line between the theoretical poles of wholly gay and wholly straight.
    With exclusive heterosexuality touted as the only normal orientation, most people

want to label themselves as normal. How fascinating that in actuality, probably only a minority could be defined as normal!

I look at why I identify myself as same-sex oriented. Is it because my strongest attractions are for my own gender? Is it because I am involved in a same-sex relationship? Is it because of a political stance? Regardless of my reasons, I am free to name my sexual identity. Others may think they know me better than I know myself, but they are wrong. I am still the expert on who I am. Today I face myself with honesty and define myself with courage. I name who I am and whom I love.

January 18 — Change

We are all likely to hold on to process until we become braver, until we dare experiment with the frightening possibilities a little at a time and a little at a time face the implications of the fact that we can change reality with incredible rapidity—instantaneously.

Sonia Johnson
Wildfire

January 19 — Change

I am transforming the world today.

Celebrating the forward motion in my life, I see a growing person with a vision that is becoming reality.

"Be patient," I have been told over and over, "Change happens slowly." A look at the progress in securing lesbian and gay rights certainly makes such statements seem true.

Change can occur quickly, too, though. History is full of discoveries and events that caused instant and far-reaching transformations. Telling me to be patient can be a way of trying to control me.

I won't be held back by people who are afraid of forward motion. I can make decisions that alter my life this very minute. What I do affects those around me, and though I cannot predict the effect, I am having an impact. With eagerness I move ahead in my quiet revolution. Impatience is my virtue today, and through it I am speeding up a sluggish world.

January 20 — Differences

In the gay rights movement, we try to emphasize that we are the same as everybody else except for what we do in bed. The American Indian cultures I studied do just the opposite; they emphasize the difference, but instead of seeing that difference as abnormal, deviant, or threatening, they see it as a "specialness," an extra gift.

Walter L. Williams
The Spirit and the Flesh

January 21   **Differences**

<u>Normal is what I decide.</u>

    Most people want to be "normal," whatever that means. I may feel more acceptable as a human being if I tell myself I am normal. I want others to like me, and I sense it as easier for people to accept those who are more like themselves than different. But my uniqueness is what makes me who I am.

    Today I look at those around me and enjoy the variety in others. They don't look "abnormal," yet each is different. I propose an exciting new concept of normal that takes in many kinds of diversity! I free myself and others from the boxes into which the world tries to force us.

    When I get the message that something is wrong with me because of my same-sex loving, I let my voice of truth drown out those oppressive ones. I celebrate everything about myself, including the wonderful way I feel about those who are my same sex. Visualizing the lesbians and gay men I know, I see their incredible beauty. They are normal, and I am normal. We are wondrously normal!

January 22   **Sexual Nurturance**

*   This is the tender inner world, the real stuff, the hush in his arms. This is nestled like a pair of spoons in the dark, waking and not wanting to part. This is the poetry one man speaks to another with his body, the love songs we have known and remember forever.*

                                                                                 Gary J. Stern
                                                            A Few Tricks Along the Way

January 23   **Sexual Nurturance**

<u>I find joy in mutual sexual nurturing.</u>

    Sex—how do I describe it for myself? Exciting, passionate, intimate, pleasureful?

    Today I explore sex as nurturing. In a culture where the model for nurturance is between parent and child, I look at the possibility of an exchange between equals. I move beyond the heterosexual mold to participate in sex as an integration of body, mind, and soul. As my lover's body interacts with mine, I allow myself the wonder of a new sensation. My energy flows to my partner and back again to the depth of my being. We give and receive in the same act of love. Our souls are fed in our physical intimacy.

    I savor this moment as pure and healthy. Its naturalness is clear. I travel beyond the triteness of a superficial world. What joy to find this wholeness of experience at an unexpected moment!

January 24   **Self-Love**

*   To love oneself is the beginning of a lifelong romance.*

                                                                                  Oscar Wilde

January 25   **Self-Love**

<u>Love for who I am moves steadily throughout my being.</u>
    I am the love of my life. As with the shyness of a new lover, I explore how best to love myself.
    At times I am discouraged by how slowly this love grows. I appreciate that I love myself more now than earlier in my life, but the self-hate instilled in me, especially because of my sexual identity, is hard to erase.
    I look for small victories today. Even in seemingly insignificant situations, affirming myself builds on a process that makes bigger steps easier. Each time I am able to accept a compliment or avoid putting myself down, my self-love grows. I let myself feel good about the parts of me I love right now, no matter how minor they seem.
    Every minute I am loving myself more. I don't have to do it all at once.

January 26   **Silence**

    I've learned in my adult life that the will to silence the truth is always and everywhere as strong as the truth itself, and so it is a necessary fight we will always be in: those of us who struggle to understand our truths and those who try to erase them.
    The first Nazi Book burning, I would have you remember, was a gay and lesbian archive.

                                                                                                      Paul Monette
                                                                                           The New York Times

January 27   **Silence**

<u>I consider silence breaking in my life.</u>
    What am I longing to tell the world? I have important information to share.
    A friend says to me, "I didn't get any negative messages about lesbians and gay men when I was growing up—I didn't even know homosexuality existed until I was 21!"
    What a powerful message I get from silence! If no one talks about being homosexual, it either isn't worthy of mention or is unspeakable in its repulsiveness. My mute culture is discounting me, condemning me, or both.
    It is painful when my friends and family who know my sexual orientation don't talk about it. They deny my reality when they ask about my "friend" who is really my lover. I, too, am often tempted to join the conspiracy of silence.
    I have the choice of speaking out, even when my words make others uncomfortable. It is not my duty to ease other people's lives at my own expense. I can throw off society's unwritten gag rule whenever I am ready and speak my truth for all to hear, including me!

January 28 — Accepting Feelings

These are the feelings I am in touch with today: _____
_____
_____
_____ It is all right to feel the way I do.

January 29 — Accepting Feelings

My feelings are right for me today.

My feelings aren't good or bad—they just are. I breathe deeply and let myself experience whatever emotions are within me this very moment.

"Count your blessings," people say to me, but sometimes my problems overwhelm me and the good parts of my life seem insignificant. What if I don't want to count my blessings?

Sometimes I need to feel dissatisfied. No one can deny the obstacles all human beings face, and my sexual orientation "blesses" me with a whole other set of hurdles. I won't shame myself when I feel depressed. It's all right to be sad, and I need to treat myself gently. If such feelings become more than I can handle, I have the courage to ask for help, but when I am going through temporary discouragement or frustration, I let myself be.

In my heart I know I am growing healthier each day; I am learning to appreciate all that happens, both positive and negative. Looking back on struggles in my past, I see how I've grown stronger and wiser by moving through them. I may not see that process happening with today's difficulties, but I am confident it is occurring. If I can't see any reason to be thankful today, I won't deny how I feel. There is a lesson to learn from every emotion. I can be grateful some other day!

January 30 — Inner Voice

People said that the Bible said homosexuals were sick and yet I knew I wasn't sick and I knew the Reality within me not only accepted but embraced my life as God-given.
Reverend Phea Y. Miller
"Two Stones and One Bird"
Our Right to Love

January 31 — Inner Voice

I listen to my inner truth.

A voice within me has important messages. I pay attention to my wise words. I may have been indoctrinated in the teachings of a certain church or the preachings of a religious leader. Some claim that the Bible or the Pope is infallible. What do I do when their words tell me I am evil? The Bible also says that God is love. How can I be evil for loving or for being the person I was born to be? When outside voices clash with what I know to be true within me, I need to listen to myself.

I embrace a higher power that speaks through my mind and heart rather than by way of external authorities. There may be those around me who have wisdom I can adopt, but only I can decide what is right for me. Perhaps I need to write a gospel according to me!

Adopting someone else's answers seems easier, but my personal revelations, tempered by the insights of those I trust and repect, are the only ones that completely fit for me. I feel a peacefulness when I work through my own belief system, and look within for my own words of truth.

February

February 1   **Self-Acceptance**

There are some people living their lives as homosexuals who would be happier if they realized they are heterosexuals. There are some people living their lives as heterosexuals who would be happier if they realized and accepted the fact that they are homosexuals. But everyone will be happier accepting himself as he is in the present and letting the future take care of itself.

Peter Fisher
The Gay Mystique

February 2   **Self-Acceptance**

I name who I truly am.

Shakespeare wrote, "That which we call a rose, by any other name would smell as sweet." When I hear people rejecting the terms "lesbian" or "gay" "queer" or "bisexual" for themselves, I agree that having a label does not make me who I am, but it can change my sense of self. I need to consider carefully how I describe myself.

What does it mean if I admit to same-sex attractions or am involved in a same-sex relationship but struggle with the possible terms? Perhaps the words seem too permanent or negative or bring to mind stereotypes that don't fit me. If I am ready to be honest with myself, though, it may be time to accept the name for the feelings within me.

Naming my sexual orientation can be an important step to developing pride within me. Do I have reservations about being labeled by my gender, my country, my religion, my profession? When I like myself just the way I am, I find words that feel comfortable and truly define who I am.

February 3 — Inner Beauty

*She who is lovely to look at is good
And she who is good shall soon be lovely as well.*

Sappho
quoted by Susan Lusk
Sappho: The Art of Loving Women

February 4 — Inner Beauty

I look beyond outward beauty.

When I visualize the "perfect" lover, is it only a body I see, or do I imagine other traits, too—the emotional, the spiritual, the mental? Living in a culture that focuses on outward appearances, I find it too easy to forget the whole person. In my same-sex loving I have the opportunity to throw off the unhealthy patterns of the mainstream world.

Although I find physical traits sexually exciting, I want a lover who is beautiful throughout. I think of the many inner qualities I want in my partner, and I envision a whole person in relationship with me. Considering what I value in friends and family, I realize how little their outer appearance affects my feelings for them. I see how the inner light creates an unmistakable radiance outside.

Today I raise my awareness and look deeply into the people I encounter. I find a new definition of beauty that opens me to the splendor of humanity.

February 5 — Self-Love

In the daily realm of love and friendship, we seldom face a zero-sum choice. The more I love you, the better able I am to love myself, and vice versa. In living this paradox, we help each other sustain creative tension between what we often think of as our own needs in relation to the needs of others.

Carter Heyward
Touching Our Strength

February 6 — Self-Love

Through self-love I free myself to love others.

I am learning how much more I bring to a relationship when I enter it with an independent sense of self. I picture strong, beautiful people loving themselves as they come together with love for each other. It is a vision of healthiness, wholeness, and giving.

rather than clinging, neediness, and dependency.
If I don't love myself, how can I reach out in love to others? If I don't consider myself worthy of my own admiration, how can I expect others to value me? If I dislike myself, I will be mistrustful of people who see me as likable. My same-sex orientation makes my self-love even more vital. When I appreciate who I am, I am more open to loving someone similar to myself.
Today I search within me for the parts of myself I can affirm. There is loveliness within me, and I embrace all of it. As I reach out to others, I keep esteem for myself very close. I am growing in love for myself and others.

February 7   **Risks of Coming Out**

The Bible says, "Do not throw your pearls before swine, lest they trample them under foot and turn to attack you." Well, my gayness is one of my treasured pearls, a pearl I own after paying a great price of personal struggle. I won't share that treasure with everybody.

Rick Cary
quoted by Ann Heron
One Teenager in Ten

February 8   **Risks of Coming Out**

<u>My coming out decisions are my own.</u>

Choosing whether to be "out" or "closeted" means weighing the need to be open against the need for self-protection. I must decide for myself whether the risks are worth taking—loss of job, gay bashing, rejection, harassment. If I find that coming out is necessary to my own sense of integrity or self-growth, I may be willing to take these risks. There will be people who criticize me whatever decision I make.
Today I consider the unique factors in my life. I can ask for advice, but no one can know what is right for me. When I center myself and let myself hear the voice of truth from within, I discover what is best for me. I am finding peace and confidence in heeding my inner truth.

February 9   **Anger**

Today I will roar like an angry lion. I will let my rage out into the universe in ways that are totally harmonious for everyone concerned.

Perry Tilleraas
The Color of Light

February 10 — Anger

My anger is an important part of me.

Anger is a sane response to the reality of my life. Dealing with the homophobic world, I feel angry. I get furious at the world that tells me I am bad and sick and defective. I am enraged when people try to change me or decide for me whether I should be in or out of the closet. I am angry with myself for not consistently standing up to the world proudly or for not always loving myself just the way I am.

Often I try to hide or deny my feelings. Today I acknowledge my anger and choose new ways of dealing with it that do not destroy myself or others. I seek people who can support me in all my emotions and places where I can express hostility safely. In certain circumstances it is inappropriate or unwise to express my anger, but I need a way to deal with all these angry feelings, and I can structure ways of doing that.

Being angry doesn't have to mean being out of control. Sometimes I need to shout my anger, but I can also be angry in a soft voice. I can find safe physical ways of dealing with strong feelings, and sometimes simply talking or crying helps me work them through.

As I deal with my anger, I am finding there is less of it, and I can live without a constant chip on my shoulder. I am being healthy in my anger.

February 11 — Higher Power

I was the only Indian in the school and had my big confrontation with the nuns when I was 6. They said that God was my father and the Virgin Mary my mother. I said, "No, that's not right. The sky is my father, the earth my mother." I was not appreciated.

Yako Myers
quoted by Mike Steele
"Caretakers of Earth"
Star Tribune, Minneapolis-St. Paul

February 12 — Higher Power

I visualize an approving higher power.

I am free to create my own theology. Many people are eager to tell me about their concepts of God. Some describe a God of the Bible who condemns me for my same-sex orientation. I have good reason to reject a deity who brought suffering upon me by creating me different. If I have had negative experiences with organized religion, the sense of a present God could seem meaningless in my life. Today I purge all the negative images I have of God and visualize a higher power that has relevance for my life, whether it is a concept of my higher self, the forces of nature, the energy that passes between people, an earth-mother goddess, or a more traditional view.

Whatever my understanding of a higher power, I know I will never have all the answers. I devise a working definition of God that makes sense to me and enhances my existence. I know my higher power approves of who I am, including my sexual orientation. If there is a creator God, then I was created good by that power, and I can live in communion with the creator. I move forward in my life, confident that the energy of the universe supports me.

February 13   **Celebrating Love**

Love, in the end, is genderless. Love is an energy that freely flows. In the end it does not matter who loves who. For the energy that fills the space between them is what matters.

Andrew Ramer
Two Flutes Playing

February 14   **Celebrating Love**
Valentine's Day

<u>I celebrate the beauty of my loving.</u>

On this holiday of love, I glory in my same-sex loving. Looking for affirmation of my love, I must go beyond the mainstream shops of cards for husbands and wives and pictures of men with women. Even valentines with teddy bears depict conspicuously heterosexual bears! How I long for images of lesbian and gay love.

When the world ignores my love, I find creative ways of affirming my relationship. I can make my own cards, write my own love poetry, seek out stores that carry items for same-sex lovers. I go to places where I can be open in my affection for my lover and choose friends who share the joy of my loving.

I revel in the beauty and naturalness of my love. Today I devise a gay jubilation of lavender hearts and rainbow lovers. Let the valentine festivities begin!

February 15   **Creating Family**

This is what I need from the people I call family: _____
_____
_____
_____
_____
_____

February 16 — Creating Family

<u>I create new family options.</u>

Family is important to me, and I choose a new definition that includes the people who continually nurture me and bring joy to my days and nights. In my same-sex orientation, I haven't always gotten what I need from my biological family.

If I have a committed partner, we are a created family. A supportive friend can substitute for a rejecting sister, brother or parent. Members of a twelve-step group or religious community may function as a new kind of family for me. Commitments with others can be unspoken or intentional.

What does "family" mean to me? I need enduring connections with people in my life. I need resources during difficult times. I need to know I matter to others.

I am innovative in my thoughts about family, discarding the old constraints that don't work for me. An exciting new definition of family is being born!

February 17 — Change for the Better

As you begin...strengthening the positive results and adjusting for the negative results, you will probably begin to notice that you produce more and more positive results for yourself. You are actually in the process of creating abundance. Being gay is becoming less of an issue to you and to those around you, and is just one more aspect of who you are.

You will still have highs and lows, but you'll begin to experience that even the negative things are better than the positive used to be.

Rob Eichberg
Coming Out—An Act of Love

February 18 — Change for the Better

<u>My life is getting better every day.</u>

Today I think of ways in which my sexual orientation has been a gift—the wisdom I have gained, the special people who might not otherwise be part of my life, the solidarity I feel with the oppressed of the world.

The difficult parts are present as well, and sometimes I feel resentful of the injustices. I keep wanting life to get easier. The important lesson, though, is that as I move through struggle after struggle, I am getting stronger and healthier. While life doesn't get easier, it gets better. I can cope with the problems and pain that I face, and I have the energy to actually enjoy life. I have the insight to appreciate its goodness and sometimes even to be grateful for its challenges.

In my moments of clarity I realize I have an important place in this world because of who I am. My destiny is to find a better life for myself and others. I am glad for my ever-improving life.

February 19 **Living with HIV/AIDS**

I listed various projects that I would like to accomplish while living proactively with AIDS and yet planning for the possibility of death.... Taking each moment as it comes, valuing and savoring it, can bring comfort, or at least exhilaration, even in the midst of suffering.

Brian Coyle
"Coming to Terms: The Coyle Journals"
Equal Time (ed. by Cynthia Scott)

February 20 **Living with HIV/AIDS**

<u>I deal with HIV.</u>

Living in this world means living with HIV. If I am not HIV-positive myself, I know people who are, and the disease is affecting all of us in some way.

If I am HIV-positive or fear being HIV-positive, I live with the reality of approaching death. Everyone dies, but many deny that reality. It is easier to deny if I don't carry a deadly virus in my body, but it is healthier to deal with the truth. I am coming to terms with my own mortality.

I know my body is capable of great healing when I summon positive energy into myself and give myself the love I deserve. As I take care of myself, I am moving toward greater healthiness.

There is time to do wonderful things in my life. I contemplate what my life work is and choose meaningful tasks that fulfill my mission. I am living one second at a time with all the energy I can bring to it. Rejoicing in my aliveness, I set about my healing and life plan.

February 21 **Fantasizing Change**

We are changes in the weather,
  we are snowflakes in July,
We are women grown together,
  we are men who easily cry,
We are words not quickly spoken,
  we're the deeper side of try,
We are dreamers in the making,
  we are not afraid of "Why?"

Ferron
"It Won't Take Long"
Shadows on a Dime [audio recording]

February 22
Presidents' Day

Fantasizing Change

I fantasize about the presidency.

Presidents' Day—yawn! It's hard to get excited about celebrating George Washington's and Abraham Lincoln's birthdays, in spite of Martin Grief's contention that George Washington "was thought by his enemies to be a bit soft on the boys and was suspected of being overly fond of [Alexander] Hamilton in particular." There is evidence that Eleanor Roosevelt shared a bed with her "friend" Lorena Hickok in the White House for several years. Others conjecture that James Buchanan, the "bachelor" president may have been lovers with his male roommate of over 20 years. The White House seems to have its share of closets.

Now if we had an openly lesbian or gay president—that would be cause to celebrate! Today I have fun fantasizing about a president who could really represent me! How about Martina Navratilova? If an actor can be president, why not a tennis player? Her partner could be referred to as the second lady, and with a little paint, they could transform their residence into the Lavender House. How about holding the inaugural ball at a gay bar? And the strides they could make on the political scene—mandating same-sex portrayals in the media for one out of every ten couples, allowing men to enter the Miss America contest, making Gay Pride Day a national holiday—the list is endless!

Wild and impossible dreams? Perhaps. But anything is possible if it can be conceived in my mind.

I let my imagination run freely today and visualize a world that affirms lesbians and gay men. I'll think gloomy thoughts some other day—for now I'm enjoying my holiday fantasy!

February 23

Valuing Self

> *I celebrate myself, and sing myself,*
> *And what I assume you shall assume,*
> *For every atom belonging to me as good belongs to you.*
> *I loaf and invite my soul.*

Walt Whitman
Song of Myself

February 24

Valuing Self

I am a treasure to be loved and prized.

Today I remind myself that I am a worthwhile, admirable person. Eleanor Roosevelt said, "No one can make you feel inferior without your consent." In a world where people try to tell me I am inferior because of my same-sex loving, I withhold my consent

to their judgment. I reach inside for the strength I need to stand up for myself.
I think about how I have been tricked into consenting to inferiority, internalizing subtle messages from my culture. I am ready to withdraw this consent. If my options appear limited, I consider new possibilites, even ones that seem unlikely or outrageous. I walk away from abusive situations, considering legal action if necessary. A look or stance can make a difference, and I give myself positive internal messages to protect myself from the negativity aimed at me. Coming out may be a way of asserting my value as a person in some situations, while staying closeted may be a valid way of avoiding harassment and maintaining a sense of dignity with those who do not understand. I choose what works for me.

I remind myself of the special qualities I possess and reaffirm that I am a valuable person. My life is a blessing to myself and others.

February 25   **Breaking Up**

> *Didn't want to say good-bye,...*
> *But you hurt me till I couldn't cry,*
> *Wouldn't cry...any longer...*
> *Now, I'm getting stronger.*
>
> Judy Fjell
> "Didn't Want to Say Good-bye"
> *Dance in the Moment* [audio recording]

February 26   **Breaking Up**

<u>I grieve over a broken relationship and open myself to healing.</u>

In ending a relationship, I take on the challenge of healing. While I can't avoid loneliness, I keep myself from becoming isolated. Some solitude is important in dealing with my pain, but connections with people are also vital to my emotional health.

As I grieve, I reach out for support. Often it is difficult to find people who can truly be there for me in this process, because of homophobia or the limited size of my community. If family, friends, or coworkers cannot give me what I need, I look for new resources. Perhaps I need friends who don't have a history with me when I was part of a couple. A professional therapist or a support group can offer different perspectives. I need sympathetic ears and safe places to let myself feel. Today I give myself permission to ask for what helps me the most.

I know I must experience my pain in order to move through it. My struggle takes me toward a time of peace and hope, even when I don't particularly feel hopeful. I take the time I need to grieve the loss of my love. As I let myself be, I come closer to serenity and a readiness to move ahead with my life.

February 27   **Honoring Love**

When I was in the military they gave me a medal for killing two men and a discharge for loving one.

Leonard Matlovich
his epitaph

February 28   **Honoring Love**

<u>My love is honorable; I rise above prejudice.</u>

    I know that my love is pure whenever I am respectful and caring, regardless of whether I love a man or a woman. I am a member of the only minority that is hated because of love. There is no logic in hating me for loving. When I see two men kissing or two women embracing, I see beauty. When I touch my lover, I sense the naturalness of our love.

    People may say I am evil, but they are evil when they deny me equal rights. Some say I am perverted, but gay bashers are perverted when they do me harm. Some still call me sick, but those who deny my personhood because of my love are sick.

    It would be easy to hate those who despise me, but today I remember the power of love. I find strength in the goodness of my same-sex loving and my confidence in its rightness for me. I find joy in my heart's messages that my love is pure and worthy of honor. I move beyond the ignorance of those who hate my loving. I can forgive them, but I assert my right to love.

March

March 1   **Coming Out**

I wish more prominent people could bring themselves to come out of their closets. Nearly always the world knows who they are already, however hard they try to fool it. Coming out would actually make their lives less isolated and troubled; it would give them faith and courage in themselves. And isn't that worth far more than the notoriety they already enjoy?

Christopher Isherwood
quoted by Leigh W. Rutledge
Unnatural Quotations

March 2   **Coming Out**

<u>I make coming-out decisions that are right for me.</u>

    Until it is equally acceptable in the world to be homosexual or heterosexual, my coming out will be a continuing part of my life, with questions I must face repeatedly. Is it time to come out to a family member? Is it wise to come out to a coworker? Will they embrace me or turn away? Will they use the information against me? If only I could anticipate how people will react! Often when I predict what someone will say and do, the exact opposite happens. It's scary, no matter how many times I go through it. I know there is always the real possibility of a negative outcome, but positive reactions can also occur.

At times I may have avoided coming out so I wouldn't hurt someone or cause a person discomfort. I remind myself that I need to make decisions based on what is important for me and let others take care of themselves. Coming out may be necessary for my own well-being, even when it causes pain to those I love. My first responsibility is to myself, and the course of action best for me will ultimately be best for those who are part of my life. Today I respect myself for the wise choices I am making.

March 3   **Positive Support**

I was lucky though to have had some women friends who were able to decode my signals, who reached out to me and encouraged me to continue to move among women. Gradually, I learned to let them in, to let them know me, to let myself be touched by them, sometimes very deeply. I am thankful for these women.

Betty Berzon
Positively Gay

March 4   **Positive Support**

<u>I seek harmony between inner and outer voices.</u>

Trusting my own judgment is vital when there are those who condemn my same-sex orientation. I also need affirmation outside myself, though. A supportive community is important to my well-being.

Seeking support doesn't mean ignoring my internal direction. It doesn't mean associating only with those who agree with me or seeking out people who encourage me in faulty thinking. If I am in denial or behaving in self-destructive ways, I need to be confronted. People who truly care about me celebrate my healthiness while challenging me to grow in areas that need change.

Finding affirmation means I don't beat myself up by listening to external messages that say I'm wrong when I know I'm right. It means I choose friends who also seek their own truth in their commitment to growth and integrity. Part of my search for the meaning of life involves putting myself in the company of people I respect and who respect me and my journey. I consider what others believe and then decide what is true for me.

Today I value my support system. As my inner voice blends with trusted voices outside, I find strength and confidence.

March 5 — Finding Community

Being gay is an adventure because there are no guidelines for living our lives. We make them up as we go along. Sometimes I wonder what will happen when society is more accepting. Will we be bound by convention? Life wouldn't be as challenging. I like being a renegade.

Richard A. Isay
quoted by Mark Thompson
Gay Soul

March 6 — Finding Community

I have fun with guessing games.

That short-haired woman in the plaid flannel shirt—could she be a lesbian? That man at the gym who seems so attentive to male bodies—is he gay? Those two women giving each other a parting embrace—could it be more than friendship? There are two male "roommates" down the hall—are they really lovers? What about the coworkers who fit the stereotype—are they or aren't they?

I let myself enjoy my amateur detective status. It is one way of reminding myself I am not alone in my same-sex orientation. If I didn't live in a homophobic culture where many lesbians and gay men stay closeted for their safety, I wouldn't have to guess. Instead, I could simply ask, as people ask whether someone is married or what a person does for a living. Even if I were universally accepted in my same-sex orientation, I would still want to know whether people I meet are potential lovers or not. Wanting people who share a commonality with me, I would still choose some lesbian and gay friends, but the search would not be clandestine or difficult.

I look forward to the time when my games are needless, but for now I find pleasure in wondering. Extending my antennae, I ferret out the "one in ten" (or more!) surrounding me. Who says only their hairdressers know for sure!

March 7 — Healing from Abuse

I've heard forever and ever, "Oh, you're a dyke because your Daddy did this to you." It's a comment that makes me mad. It's a way that people take choices away from me. Maybe if I was a murderer, you could say that was connected to the incest. If there was going to be a correlation, it would be between the incest and my capacity for violence or hatred, not with my capacity for love.

unnamed lesbian
quoted by Ellen Bass and Laura Davis
The Courage to Heal

March 8 **Healing from Abuse**

I heal from sexual abuse.

Many people, heterosexual, homosexual and bisexual, male and female, have suffered sexual abuse. Even if I have not experienced such abuse myself, someone close to me may be a survivor of abuse, and I choose to participate in the collective healing of a sick society that has allowed this violence to occur.

I need to be patient and impatient—letting myself know that the healing will take a long time while working to find the help I need to speed the healing process. Trusting my inner voice, I do whatever is necessary to take care of myself. I did not deserve this abuse. I do deserve to heal.

I realize that my sexual orientation is a positive aspect of my selfhood, not the negative after-effect of past trauma. I affirm that no one can make me homosexual or heterosexual. If I am bisexual, my life experiences may affect which gender I choose for my relationships, but when it is a choice, I am in control of that choice. As I find more joy in my same-sex loving, I refuse to give any perpetrator of evil credit for what is good in my nature. I am who I am, and I am healing with each new day.

March 9 **Defining Relationship**

Anyway I love you very much indeed, and I do propose to you now, in front of the cameras. You've had five years with me—shall we have a bash at the next five? No promises, no bargains, and we're not into revenge—that's our motto.

lesbian
Women Like Us [video]
Suzanne Neild and Rosalind Pearson

March 10 **Defining Relationship**

Vows with my partner are based on love.

With neither the privilege nor the pressure to marry legally, I am free to choose a commitment of love with my partner. Released from cultural expectations and family dictates by my same-sex orientation, I can continue in my relationship without a formal contract or decide on a unique declaration of what our relationship means to each of us.

Marriage has been used as a way of legalizing ownership of women by men. Saint Paul in the Bible instructed wives to submit to their husbands. I'm glad I am free to enter into a relationship in which my partner and I are equals. We can reject the baggage of an oppressive history and society and let each other be individuals.

Organized religion has often stressed reproduction as the purpose of marriage. My inability to have biological children with my same-sex partner frees me from accidental or socially pressured parenting. Although it becomes difficult for me to be a parent by choice in some contexts, there are options, and I rejoice that my partner and I can be intentional about being parents. Our love for each other has a depth that involves much more than a union aimed solely at procreation.

I deserve the right to a legal union with my partner, but for now I celebrate the love I offer and receive. My partner and I find our own words for the life we share.

March 11 — Inner Truth

Nobody will tell you the truth. You have to listen and you have to look because no one is going to tell you.

Audre Lorde
quoted by Amber Coverdale Sumrall
Write to the Heart

March 12 — Inner Truth

I find honest answers.

Was there a time in my life when I wanted to accept the world's easy answers as truth?

"All of us are meant to love the opposite sex."

"If I marry I can be heterosexual."

"Homosexuality is a sin."

"My same-sex attraction is just a passing phase."

I have searched my heart and mind. These answers are not true for me. The questions weren't easy—how can the answers be easy? My heart knows that easy answers don't work. I face my own honest answers:

- I am meant to love someone of my own sex, whether or not that love is accepted by others.
- I may be able to be sexual with either a man or a woman, but inside I am still the same, and people who try to change me are disrespectful.
- I was created a beautiful person, and my sexual orientation is a natural part of me, to be celebrated, not shamed.
- In my heart I know my sexual orientation, and I won't try to deny who I am.

These are the answers that speak my truth and bring an inner peace. I have slain the false dragons of easy answers.

March 13 — Death and Life

As I collected the stories of this long passage I often wept with these women as they recalled their hardships and their losses....Their vitality and strength in later life taught me that things we fear most—illness, separation from lovers and friends—can be survived; that death and dying are just another part of life.

Marcy Adelman
Long Time Passing

March 14   **Death and Life**

<u>I am learning to deal with death.</u>

    With the epidemic of AIDS, a war of disease is being waged on bodies of all ages. I am aware of the fear and foreboding it has brought. I have grieved over friends and loved ones who have passed. When I feel overwhelmed by the withered vibrancy, the unfulfilled dreams, the lost energy, I remember that these deaths help me look at the meaning of life. I resist the temptation to evade the pain as I learn the lessons it teaches. When someone close to me dies, I am faced with the reality of my own mortality. I must judge whether I am living the life I need to live for today, realizing that I too may be limited in my tomorrows.

    I am learning to say good-bys as I grow through my pain. Memories and love keep these people alive in my heart. I see how their influence on others continues, and I see their contributions making a permanent mark on the world. Little by little, I am coming to terms with death as part of the cycle of life whenever it occurs, and I am learning to live one day at a time.

March 15   **Healthy Sexuality**

    Straights can learn a lot from us gay people. We teach straight people so many things about sexuality. Like, perhaps, not to take it quite so seriously...not to kill each other over it.

                                                                                         Armistead Maupin
                                                                             quoted by Leigh W. Rutledge
                                                                                   Unnatural Quotations

March 16   **Healthy Sexuality**

<u>I claim healthy sexuality for myself.</u>

    My sexuality is an important part of my life, enhancing many areas: pleasure, intimacy, nurturance, spirituality. Living in a sex-obsessed culture, however, I must work hard to be healthy in my sexuality. Advertisers use sex to sell products from toothpaste to chain saws. Jokes about sex debase its sacredness. Swearing without using sexual terms is nearly impossible.

    Because I am attracted to my own sex, I have to deal with people who want to define me purely in terms of my sexuality. I must confront the myths that homosexuals think of nothing but sex and that we want to have physical intimacy with everyone of the same gender. I explore whether I have internalized any of these beliefs unknowingly. Moving beyond all the unhealthiness around me, I seek a sexuality that is natural for me.

    I reject the easy ways out—giving in to stereotypes and overemphasizing sex, or avoiding sex and feeling shame when my sexuality emerges. Listening to my inner voice, I bring my life into balance. As I discover an expanding range of pleasure within as well as beyond my sexuality, I rejoice in the health and wholeness that is mine.

March 17 — Diversity of Age

But in between the laughter and the stories told and untold, I discerned the advice and experience of my surrogate uncles. Today I see this verbal odyssey for what it was: a journey within and beyond myself; a series of conversations with men who, as I grow older, become younger and younger to me.

Boze Hadleigh
Conversations with My Elders

March 18 — Diversity of Age

<u>I enrich my life by reaching out to persons of all ages.</u>

I'm drawn to people like myself for the affirmation they give me, but sometimes I forget that I also need people different from myself to appreciate the diversity of my world. I want the dreams and wisdom of people both younger and older than myself to enrich me. For a healthy perspective, I need to touch the beginning and ending of life, as well as all the moments in between.

In my same-sex orientation, it is easy to become isolated from people of varying ages. Society's tendency to label me as a child molester may make me hesitant to spend time with children. Finding older lesbians and gay men is sometimes difficult, and I may hesitate to be open with older straight people because of my assumptions about their attitudes toward homosexuality. Having suffered rejection in the past, I may find it hard to reach out to people regardless of their age or attitudes.

As part of the whole human family, I won't let my sexual orientation make my connections with others less than all-encompassing. Looking at the diversity of ages around me, I invite that diversity into my life. There are lessons for me to learn from everyone, and I offer my gifts for others' lives. I open myself to the abundance of humanity.

March 19 — Spring and Growth

My greatest joy in life is recognizing how much I have changed for the better and how much more growth I have before me.

Brian McNaught
A Disturbed Peace

March 20 — Spring and Growth
Vernal Equinox

<u>New beginnings in my life are springtimes of growth.</u>

As spring unfolds once more into my life, I visualize coming out to those I care about as a springtime in my relationships. Coming out is always a risk, but when I am able to take that step, it signals a time of new honesty and new learning. The possibility of new intimacy is also real. If I am rejected because of my sexual orientation, I am able to move on to new relationships, and I feel a deeper peace with myself as my sense of integrity increases.

I cannot have a truly honest relationship with anyone who does not know my sexual orientation. There will be topics I have to avoid or talk around. With some, I may choose such a relationship, but I treasure being able to be completely open with those who are important to me. When I can reveal my truth, I grow like the tender spring bulbs opening into the crisp spring mornings.

Today I celebrate the advent of spring—in nature and in my coming-out process. I approach the seasons of my life with resilience and hope.

March 21   Spring
Vernal Equinox

I think of a time that was a new beginning in my life. I think of how I felt then: _____

_____

_____

This is how my feelings have changed: _____

_____

_____

March 22   Happiness

I finally figured out the only reason to be alive is to enjoy it.

Rita Mae Brown
quoted by Amber Coverdale Sumrall
Write to the Heart

March 23   Happiness

<u>As I find happiness for myself, I help others in their quest.</u>

I deserve to be happy, and I am discovering the wisdom of giving my own happiness first priority. I was raised to give the happiness of others greater importance than my own. If I put myself first, I was told I was selfish. When I got in touch with my same-sex orientation, I was condemned for desiring a natural pleasure. As I experience my living, however, I find that when I ignore what makes me happy, I make those around me as miserable as I am. In taking care of myself, I support the needs of others better.

What a joy that I don't have to make a choice between myself and others! The way to help others be happy is to find my own happiness. Taking care of myself is the most important thing I can do for those around me.

I banish feelings of guilt when I fulfill my needs and wants. As I love myself, I am loving the universe. Today I seek my own happiness and sense my harmony with the world.

March 24 — Strength

Sisters and Brothers, we stand united
The flame of hope has been ignited
The flame burns bright, it lights the skies
And in my heart, I know we'll rise
We will rise, We will rise, we will rise...

Joseph Victor Sieger
"We Will Rise"
Self Portrait, 1993 [audio recording]

March 25 — Strength

I love the strength within me.

What a strong person I have become! Sometimes I would rather forget the pain and struggle that have contributed to my strength. Sometimes the homophobic world does not appreciate who I have become. But here I am—a powerful, determined survivor!

I have triumphed over oppression, abuse, conflict, challenges—I am truly amazing! Taking a long look at myself, I see my lovely emotional muscles. My self-admiration is well-deserved. I have many wonderful qualities, but today I especially appreciate my strength.

March 26 — Sexual Orientation

I tried to persuade myself that I was three-quarters normal and that only a quarter of me was queer—whereas really it was the other way round.

W. Somerset Maugham
quoted by Leigh W. Rutledge
Unnatural Quotations

March 27   **Sexual Orientation**

<u>I face my true sexual orientation.</u>

    An adolescent prays persistently, "God, make me straight." In struggling with my same-sex orientation, I too have longed to be acceptable, but trying to change myself is not the answer.

    My sexual orientation is a core part of me. If I am actually bisexual, then being "cured" of homosexuality is not really changing who I am but merely focusing on a part of myself I wish to develop. If the predominant part of me is same-sex oriented, I may be able to change how I act or don't act, but it does not change who I am.

    I know myself better than anyone else in this world, and I know how strong my same-sex orientation is. Today I meditate on who I am rather than who the world wants me to be. As I listen to my heart and celebrate its goodness, I set the direction for my life.

March 28   **Commitment**

*   But the fear of intimacy lingers. We can only hope that our quick maturation, and our evolving understanding of commitment and relationship will give us the faith in one another that comes with time, and the consequent security that will permit us to enjoy the intimacy we have earned in this process of helping one another to live and die.*

                                                                                                                   Don Clark
                                                                          The New Loving Someone Gay

March 29   **Commitment**

<u>I create healthy options in my love relationships.</u>

    When traditional relationship patterns are irrelevant to my same-sex loving, I free myself to find new ways of being. The mainstream community sets me up by denying me the option of legal marriage and then condemning me for being "promiscuous." Being raised in a culture that idealizes marriage as the only approved relationship, I may be tempted to go to the extreme of not making any commitments. Commitment is scary at best, and it is harder for me when I am outside the mainstream.

    Today I recognize that I don't have to be limited or controlled by my culture. When I am caring and responsible in my love relationships, I have made a commitment—even if I don't have a spoken agreement or a ceremony.

    Taking time to explore what I want in my relationship, I risk discussing the possibilities with my lover. I am a moral person and I define what that means to me. I am a mature person, and I consider how that affects my interactions. I am a loving person, and I look at how intimacy and commitment inter-relate in my life. Casting off the outmoded and irrelevant, I am free to devise a new model of being together.

March 30   **Choices**

Of course I didn't have to talk about my sexual preference in public. Of course taking on any label is self-limiting and wrong. But that's not the point. Because of my homosexuality I can't get a job as a coach. Unless certain attitudes change there's no way for me to function in this society doing what I want to do. If some of us don't take on the oppressive labels and publicly prove them wrong, we'll stay trapped by the stereotypes for the rest of our lives.

Dave Kopay
quoted by Leigh W. Rutledge
Unnatural Quotations

March 31   **Choices**

<u>I take care of myself around homophobic people.</u>

    Straight people aren't "out" all the time (aside from society's assumptions), and I don't need to be either. When I feel it is in my best interest to stay closeted but can't speak honestly without coming out, what do I do?

    My integrity is important, but at times I must also consider protecting myself. The more I, along with other lesbians and gay men, have the courage to be out, the sooner the world will truly accept us. I can't live my whole life as a political being, though. My decisions must reflect what is best for me.

    No solution is inherently right or wrong. Every decision I make is the wisest possible one for the situation at that time. Today I consider carefully how I interact with homophobic people. My choices are valid for me.

April

April 1   **Lightening Up**
April Fool's Day

But I choose humor because laughter breaks down barriers. Laughter cuts through stereotypes; it gives us a break from the all-too-real heterosexist oppression out there. But mostly, humor gives us hope: hope for a better future for all of us.

Ellen Orleans
Can't Keep a Straight Face

<u>I am learning to laugh at myself.</u>

    Today I look for the humor in who I am. I am not making fun of myself in a derogatory way or putting myself down, but I laugh at my mistakes, my inconsistencies, even my gullibility at falling for tricks.

If I fear being laughed at for being different, I am tempted to try to be like those around me. In coming to a realization of my same-sex orientation, I have known that to be different often means being hated and treated unfairly. But I have never lost my sense of humor.

As I grow in wisdom, I come to understand conformity as a trap. I can never be like everyone else, because each person is different. In my heart I know the goodness of diversity. When I celebrate my differences, even laugh at them sometimes, I live in this world more successfully.

I am not a "fool"—I have intelligence—but sometimes I take myself too seriously. On this holiday of humor, I laugh at myself, I lighten up, I celebrate the fact that life is fun and funny, even *my* life!

April 2 **Overcoming Depression**

Some people are defeated by life. Others survive and flourish against all odds. What tips the balance is the drive to change our circumstances, to take fate on a dare and make of our lives what we want them to be.

Gary J. Stern
A Few Tricks Along the Way

April 3 **Overcoming Depression**

I deal with depression.

It is normal to be depressed at times. I do not need to label myself as sick or mentally unstable when I feel depressed. I let myself feel whatever feelings are real for me today, and I am gentle with myself. Whether I am reacting to issues related to my same-sex orientation or to other situations, feeling depressed at times is inescapable.

I let myself feel depressed if that is what I need to do, but I also make changes that increase my level of satisfaction. I know I have control over many aspects of my life. The alternatives may be ones I prefer not to choose, but as I recognize that I do have choices, my depression lessens.

Taking control of my life means looking at options creatively and formulating plans that will get me where I want to be. Even if the step is small, I make some move toward getting there. If I need to, I ask for help, and I reach out to those who can provide support. I deserve to be happy, and that's exactly where I'm headed!

April 4   **Being Out at Work**

This is my fantasy of a homophobia-free workplace: _____

_____

_____

_____

_____

April 5   **Being Out at Work**

<u>I make wise decisions in my workplace.</u>

    I look carefully at how out I am ready to be at work. When people still can be fired because of their sexual orientation, staying closeted may be in my best interests, but it is never easy. No one has the right to tell me how to live my life.
    Even if I don't have to fear being fired over my sexual orientation, I may decide not to come out if I anticipate abusive treatment or being shunned. If I am ready, I can decide to challenge any would-be tormentors. I know there are rewards and risks in whatever I choose.
    Any course of action takes courage, and my efforts in dealing with prejudice are helping to create a world of justice and love. Each day brings choices and decisions, and I am finding new ways of dealing with these challenges.
    As I visualize better tomorrows, I live in the today that is. My mind is at peace. I am doing what is best for me.

April 6   **Supporting Relationship**

*   Friends who get the word on the grapevine start phoning one or the other of us and tell us we're a great match. We agree that I can tell our mutual physician at my next visit, and she beams at the news. I bask in the sense of community support. I love seeing my friends light up in response to my happy face.*

                                                      Jeanne Adleman
                                            quoted by Marcy Adelman
                                                         Long Time Passing

April 7   **Supporting Relationship**

<u>I affirm my love relationship.</u>

    I need support for the relationship I share with my lover. Whether I am open about my same-sex loving or not, the negative homophobic messages are easy to internalize.

If I am closeted, not celebrating my love in all areas of my life carries the implication that I am ashamed of my relationship.

I may fool myself into believing my partner and I can be self-sufficient—that our love can survive without outside affirmation—but I know in my heart I need reminders that my love is special and good. Having others who are happy for my partner and me helps us sustain our caring.

Today I consider new possibilities in finding encouragement for my loving. I connect with people who help me celebrate my relationship. Reaching deeply into my heart, I find pride in my caring. Hiding my love at times does not mean I am ashamed of it. My love deserves to shine in the light, and I am bringing a glow to it from both inside and outside our togetherness.

April 8   **Stereotypes**

Being gay means having freed oneself of misgivings over being homosexual. At its best it means not limiting oneself to a stereotype—a model of some previous homosexual—for one's personality, at work, at parties, with a lover. It means remaining free to invent, to imbue life with fantasy. It means being able to investigate one's preferences and desires in sexual roles where one chooses, without having to construct a personality elsewhere consistent with this, to justify it, to account for it. In essence, it means being convinced that any erotic preference may be housed in any human being.

George Weinberg
Society and the Healthy Homosexual

April 9   **Stereotypes**

<u>I move beyond stereotypes.</u>

I am ready to be my own person. Putting other people in boxes puts me in a box too. It may feel comfortable in a box, but it limits me. Whether I want to appear straight or gay, I need to resist the temptation to take on any particular stereotype unthinkingly. I concentrate on simply being myself, throwing off the subtle messages I have internalized from my culture of what I am expected to be.

I am more than a label, more than a stereotype, more than words can describe—ever changing and growing, unpredictable, unlimited in potential and beauty.

I can fit in without trying to be the same as others in my peer group. Even if I look or act differently from those around me, there will always be those comfortable enough with themselves to accept me.

Exploring the uniqueness within me, I find what feels right and celebrate my being. I am a new edition, a signed original, a one-of-a-kind. I am wonderful, beautiful ME!

April 10   **Self-Affirmation**

I believe that all sexuality is a gift from God. And since God doesn't make junk, being gay is wonderful. We all need to feel good about ourselves, don't we?

Father Robert L. Arpin
Wonderfully, Fearfully Made

April 11   **Self-Affirmation**

I am a beautiful part of the universe.

The Bible says God surveyed all of creation and saw that it was good; that goodness includes me. I know I was created to be exactly as I am and that my sexual orientation is a natural and lovely part of me, despite others' attempts to pronounce me evil or perverted. Now I find affirmation in the very Bible that has been used to condemn my same-sex loving.

As I come to trust myself more and more, I let myself know that I am a good person and that my capacity to love someone of the same sex is an important part of my beauty. The universe was created as it is meant to be. I am who I was intended to be. I feel in harmony with my higher power, and I let that sense of my beauty fill my being.

April 12   **Anger**

One of the greatest challenges that has always faced the lesbian and gay community has been how to deal creatively and productively with all the anger that necessarily results from our frequent alienation from family, church, and society.

John J. McNeil
Taking a Chance on God

April 13   **Anger**

I deal constructively with my anger.

Anger serves a useful purpose. I may try to deny my feelings of anger. It can be frightening and may control me, as well as others, at times. Today I recognize anger's value and look at how I can use it effectively.

I learn from the way a gardener handles thistles invading a garden. The thistles intimidate with their thorns, they choke out more fragile plants, they survive all manner of adversity. The gardener who tries to eradicate them through brute force breaks the stalk but leaves the root which quickly regenerates itself. In contrast, the gardener who exerts slow, careful pressure uproots the entire plant, and the thistle withers, losing its power.

In dealing with a hostile, maddening world, I am like the wise gardener. I control my anger and use it positively, working with calculated persistence. Through my determined anger, I am bringing about change. Within myself, transformation is also occurring. As I use my energy to work for good, my own pain is eased. I am healing the world and myself through my anger.

April 14 — Not Needing Reasons

I ascertain that I'm homosexual. OK. That's no cause for alarm. How and why are idle questions. It's a little like my wanting to know why my eyes are green.

Jean Genet
quoted by Leigh W. Rutledge
Unnatural Quotations

April 15 — Not Needing Reasons

<u>I am who I am.</u>

People who believe my same-sex loving is abnormal keep trying to find reasons for the way I am. They don't want to believe I could be born this way and that I am perfectly normal.

Sexual abuse, negative experiences with the opposite sex, a domineering mother, a passive or non-present father, arrested sexual development, mental illness, "settling" for same-sex relationships because of unattractiveness—such creative nonsense!

I don't need a reason for my same-sex attractions. I don't care if I was born as I am or have developed my attractions. It doesn't matter if I made a conscious choice or feel my orientation was created within me. I certainly have had negative experiences in my life, but they didn't "make" me homosexual!

Today I celebrate who I am without asking why or trying to explain. Straight people don't try to figure out why they are heterosexual. I am fine just the way I am, and my same-sex loving is healthy, natural, and wonderful. It is, I accept it, and I rejoice in it!

April 16 — Loving Self and Others

I do not need to let a straight person make me feel inferior because I am not straight.

I do not need to try to make a straight person feel inferior because she or he is not gay.

I do not need to let another gay person make me feel inferior because I am not the same kind of gay person she or he is.

I can make my own choices about everything.

Mel White
The Dyke Daily Companion

April 17   **Loving Self and Others**

<u>My self-love sustains itself.</u>

    I see others putting people down in a seeming attempt to build themselves up—such a shabby way of treating people! I know that hating others doesn't generate love for myself.
    Some heterosexuals assume that homosexuals hate those of the opposite sex, but I can love myself and also respect and love those who are different from me. I relate to those of the opposite sex even if I don't choose them as lovers. Including people of both sexes in my living creates balance; excluding people from certain aspects of my life isn't the same as hating them.
    Today I consider what helps me feel good about myself and my same-sex orientation. I seek support for who I am in positive ways without oppressing others. My focus is on love, not hate, and I let that love bring serenity and greater self-esteem into my being.

April 18   **Accepting Life Process**

What a wonderful life I've had! I only wish I'd realized it sooner.
                                                                                                Colette
                                                     quoted by Amber Coverdale Sumrall
                                                                     Write to the Heart

April 19   **Accepting Life Process**

<u>I celebrate knowing and accepting my sexual orientation.</u>

    I think back to when I didn't admit to my same-sex orientation. There were clues I ignored, signs I didn't want to see. In getting to this place, I have experienced pain and will go through more pain in my life struggles, but I have the wholeness of truly knowing and accepting myself for who I am. I treasure the peace I have found in coming to terms with my sexual orientation.
    It's easy to wish I had come to terms with myself sooner. How much loving did I miss because of my resistance? Have I "wasted" a significant part of my life?
    Today I let myself know I am always at the point in my life where I need to be. A coming-out process takes time, and I let myself be wherever I am in that process for now. I enjoy knowing who I am, not worrying about who I was or will become.
    I'm doing just fine, and I celebrate my journey this very minute, progressing at the very best speed.

April 20 Caring

No partner in a love relationship should feel that she has to give up an essential part of herself to make it viable.

May Sarton
quoted by Amber Coverdale Sumrall
Write to the Heart

April 21 Caring

I create a new model of caring.

I want to be caring in my relationships. In a culture that encourages over-dependency, I must work to avoid that kind of behavior with the significant people in my life.

Today I look at ways I may have fostered unhealthy dependency in caring for those around me—pressuring them to "do it my way," doing things for people who are perfectly capable of acting for themselves, prying into aspects of people's lives that are not my business, being overconcerned about other people.

In my same-sex loving, I am a trailblazer in many areas, and this is one more way I can be involved in healthy change. The heterosexual norms don't apply to my life, and I gladly reject the destructive patterns I see around me. I develop better ways of relating—respecting others' independence, supporting those I care about without taking over their lives, allowing others their privacy, recognizing others' capabilities, and having confidence in their capacity to be in control of their lives.

My trailblazing is a challenge. Imitation is much simpler, but I choose to live creatively. Today I show caring without smothering. I love the special people in my life with a new healthiness.

April 22 Miracles

We must envision the world we want, make it so real in our hearts that it already exists like the child growing towards birth, while we shape our songs of encouragement.

Elsa Gidlow
"Footprints in the Sands of Time"
Sinister Wisdom

April 23 Miracles

I open myself to the miraculous in my life.

In this age of science, there isn't much understanding of the nature of miracles. Facing many hurdles in the way of my same-sex orientation, I find it especially tempting to be cynical and conclude that even if miracles happen for some people, they won't happen for me.

I open my mind and let myself think of experiences that cannot be readily explained in terms of conventional thinking. Perhaps I need to redefine the word "miracle" in a way that fits my life, or find a different word to describe realities that seem to defy logic. I know I can't explain everything that happens in this world according to scientific laws, academic rationality, or empirical data.

My outlook on life affects what happens to me. With confidence I embrace the possibilities of positive energy. I deserve to have good things happen to me. Even if it seems preposterous or unlikely, I visualize what I would like for myself. Good things are taking place in my life constantly, especially when I am open to them. A miracle is occurring this very day for me—I am ready to let it happen!

April 24   **Sexuality Definitions**

There exists today a pressing personal need for us to reclaim that which is life-enhancing and lovely within the "lesbian" and "gay" community. Yet we have, I think, a simultaneous need to dive down deep, to risk, to question, to continually challenge the old terms, assumptions, and institutions, to radically remake the meaning of our lives and restructure the social organization of our bodies.

Jonathan Katz
Gay/Lesbian Almanac

April 25   **Sexuality Definitions**

<u>I am evolving, as I define words that apply to who I am.</u>

Words regarding my sexual self whirl about me: "sexual identity," "sexual preference," "sexual orientation," "sexuality." What do they mean to me? As I contemplate the different terms, I explore my place in the universe and how I relate to those in the life-process with me.

Some speak of my same-sex attractions as my sexual preference, but if I believe I was born to love those of the same sex, the word preference mistakenly implies a choice. If people talk of my sexual identity in terms of homosexuality, they assume my same-sex loving is the totality of my sexual identity, when in truth my sexual identity also includes my concept of myself as belonging to my gender and a sense of what maleness and femaleness means, as well as how I fit or don't fit into my gender role culturally. My sexuality involves same-sex loving but also includes my view of myself as a sexual being and how I relate to both women and men within that stance. The term "sexual orientation" allows me to categorize my same-sex loving without judging or excluding other areas of sexuality and sexual identity.

The "truths" I was told as I grew up mean little or nothing to me now. I need to find my own definitions or recognize that life is a constant redefining of terms, all on many continuums: male-female, gay-straight, sexual-asexual, masculine-feminine. My definition may be to say definitions are useless.

My meanings tomorrow will be different from those of today. I am an ever-changing being, and my dictionary is a technicolor movie, not a black and white snapshot!

April 26   **Balance in Relationships**

Laura: During the seventh year of the relationship we almost broke up. What made the difference was the help of some friends who gave us a different perspective on the relationship and the difficulties we were experiencing.
Robin: Our friends came and said, "You can't do this to us."
Laura: "You can't do it. If you think you really want to break up, you have to sit down and talk to us."
Robin: They made us make contracts with each other. And we did.
Susan: How loving.
Robin: Yes. We were really fortunate.

lesbian couple
quoted by Susan E. Johnson
Staying Power

April 27   **Balance in Relationships**

<u>I nurture all my relationships.</u>

When I am in a relationship with a single partner, I sometimes am tempted to neglect friendships and other sources of support, expecting my partner to meet all my needs.

My well-being is enhanced by having a wide circle of relationships and a variety of experiences. No one person can be everything to me. Expecting too much from one person places stress on our relationship. I want to stay healthy in all areas of my life, and that involves seeking balance.

Today I evaluate the important relationships in my life. I consider which ones need more attention. If my partner has restricted relationships, perhaps we can discuss the situation together and plan how each of us can reach outside without hurting the other. Without waiting for a crisis to force change, I work actively for what is healthy and balanced. I am making wise decisions in all my relationships. The energy I give nurtures myself and those I love.

April 28   **Rightness of My Loving**

Mommy says Daddy and Frank are gay. At first I didn't know what that meant. So she explained it. Being gay is just one more kind of love.

Michael Wilhoite
Daddy's Roommate

April 29   **Rightness of My Loving**

<u>I am beautiful in my same-sex loving.</u>
    Love is the positive energy of the universe. Nothing can negate the virtue of my loving—not silence, not invisibility, not oppression. If there were no other same-sex couples in the world, my love would still be right. If all same-sex loving were banished, my longings would still be worthy. The zealots of the world cannot take away what I know to be true. When my love for another honors both of us, we are deserving of reverence from all around us. If that acceptance is denied, I let the love I feel for others flow back to me in love for myself. I am beautiful because I love. My radiance shines forth.

April 30   **Chemical Dependency**

*   Many of us know the place we start from, but none of us know how far we will go along the way. For all of us, recovery is the greatest adventure of our lives, and we each reach far beyond anything we ever knew or expected with every step we take.*
                                                                                        Sheppard Kominars
                                                                                        Accepting Ourselves

May

May 1   **Chemical Dependency**

<u>I am committed to healthiness.</u>
    The statistics on chemical dependency among lesbians and gay men are telling. As a member of an oppressed minority, I struggle to be emotionally healthy in spite of discrimination. Turning to chemicals for comfort is a constant temptation, since I find easy access to prescription and non-prescription drugs, alcohol, cigarettes, or simply coffee.
    I have many challenges in my life, but I can deal with them in healthful ways. I don't have to become a statistic, and I can react to stress by becoming strong, not weak. The good feelings I find in chemical use are transient and may in time become debilitating. The sense of well-being I seek is based on healthful, authentic living. If keeping myself away from such chemicals for all of today seems too hard, I commit to the next minute. I take small steps, one at a time, one after another. When I need help, I ask for it—from friends and family, through professional treatment, in support groups.
    Today I look at constructive ways of dealing with the difficult parts of my life. I remind myself of all the struggles I have successfully weathered. Having made it this far with grace, I am going much further. I center myself and summon the strength within me. By choosing to be more chemical-free, I am taking care of myself. I deserve the best, and that is what I'm giving myself.

May 2 — Accepting Compliments

Here are some compliments I deserve: _____

_____

_____

_____

May 3 — Accepting Compliments

I accept affirmation of myself from others.

I look at the different levels of credibility I give to positive or negative comments people give me. Why is it so much easier to believe the bad things that are said than the good things? I often dismiss compliments as meaningless or insignificant. Sometimes I even turn them into negatives—if she thinks I look nice today, does she really mean I usually look terrible?

With society's obstacles to my same-sex orientation, the tendency to absorb criticism is even stronger. The world has been pronouncing me "bad" for so long, I expect the negative. I've been trained well.

I am ready to reverse my pattern. I look with skepticism on negative comments, not automatically assuming they are true. When it fits, I accept honest, constructive criticism and greet it as an opportunity to grow and improve. If an evaluation is unfair, I reject it. I know myself well, and I decide what is true for me. Considering whether a source is trustworthy, I shield myself against unkindness or hurtfulness.

On the other side, I accept sincere compliments graciously and let myself really hear them. There is a lot about me to admire. I let others show that admiration and I feel the glow deep within. The good stuff is really true!

May 4 — Enjoying the Outrageous

I became not merely a self-confessed homosexual, but a self-evident one. That is to say I put my case not only before the people who knew me but also before strangers. This was not difficult to do. I wore makeup at a time when even on women eye shadow was sinful....From that moment on, my friends were anyone who could put up with the disgrace....To survive at all was adventure; to reach old age was a miracle.

Quentin Crisp
The Naked Civil Servant

May 5 — Enjoying the Outrageous

I savor the thrills of my controversial loving.

My same-sex orientation gives new meaning to the term "forbidden fruit"! As long as I can't get the Good Housekeeping Seal of Approval for who I am, I might as well enjoy the life of a renegade. I feel glee in kissing a lover behind someone's back, or, if I am a true rebel, I delight in shocking strangers with public passion. Even in privacy, I find subtle excitement in committing the outrageous. If I can't always keep the world out of my bedroom, at least I can provide a spectacular show! Someday my same-sex love will be part of the mainstream, and I may be ready to be less than flamboyant, but for now I am leading a revolution of the heart, in and out of the closet!

May 6 — Building Relationship

And now begins a time when not only do we arouse and satisfy passion in each other, we also read poetry, tell stories of our lives, and talk, talk, talk. With this intensity, intimacy is building.

Jeanne Adleman
quoted by Marcy Adelman
Long Time Passing

May 7 — Building Relationship

I become healthier in my relationships each day.

How can I have good intimate relationships if I don't have role models I trust and admire? I see unhealthy coupling all around me, but learning what *not* to do still doesn't tell me what *to do*. Since my same-sex loving lacks tradition and long-standing cultural norms to fall back on, I create new patterns in process with a lover.

I have good ideas, common sense, and a deep desire to be respectful in my loving. Through trial and error I am developing new ways of being together with a lover. Each experience brings learning and growth.

What wonderful irony—while the world is busy condemning my same-sex loving, I am putting my energy into creating a more constructive model of intimacy than most heterosexuals have even dreamed of. I am building a radical new world that starts with the love I share.

May 8   **Self-Disclosure**

I wish that homosexuals were born with a little horn in the middle of their forehead so we couldn't hide so easily. At least if you can't hide, you have to stand up and fight.

Harvey Fierstein
quoted by Leigh W. Rutledge
Unnatural Quotations

May 9   **Self-Disclosure**

<u>I keep only the masks that are wisely worn.</u>

    Everyone has masks, and some are healthy. Self-disclosure can be wise or foolhardy. In my same-sex loving, I may have more masks than heterosexuals in order to protect myself, but I need to be my real self for my inner peace and an honest connection with those I love.

    Masks may feel familiar and safe, but they are not always necessary. If I am not being open with my family members, I evaluate whether it is for their benefit or mine. If I consider a mask important at work, I look at what other options are open to me. When I continue being closeted with straight friends because I fear losing their friendship, I must deal with the fact that the depth of those friendships will be limited when I hide my sexual orientation.

    I face my fear that people will reject me if I am open, and weigh it against my dislike of pretending to be someone I'm not. Today I study the masks I wear and decide if I am ready to discard any of them. I hold onto those that are helpful, discarding with courage the ones I no longer need.

May 10   **Spirituality**

We are all spiritual beings striving to unfold our power and perfection, whether we are aware of it or not.

Roger Lanphear
Gay Spirituality

May 11   **Spirituality**

<u>My spirituality is part of who I am.</u>

    I claim a wholeness that encompasses the depth of my soul. If I rejected the religious community of my childhood because it denounced my sexual orientation, that doesn't mean I have to deny my spiritual nature. I affirm my spirituality by seeing it as part of my own being, not the creation of oppressive religious institutions. Today I find ways of validating the holiness within my life. I can have religious experiences alone or with others outside of any organized community of faith. If I choose, I am free to visualize a higher power as the life energy within my being or as a force outside myself. I can find deity in a sunset across a lake or in a city alley. As I test new paradigms, I gain wisdom that adds meaning and fullness to my life.

If I long for a spiritual community, I know groups that can affirm me. A lesbian/gay church, synagogue or coven offers tradition and support. Twelve-step groups provide an approach with a less structured theology. Even groups with no religious ties can have spiritual elements.

My connection with the universe is the core of my being, and the energy of that bond is growing stronger. I rejoice in the sacred within me, as the sense of my completeness flows throughout my being.

May 12   **Growth Through Pain**

You began to see, and even rejoice to see, what you always saw. You can even tell anguish to sit down, and shut up, you're busy right now—and anguish, as you should certainly know by now, ain't to go nowhere. It might go around the corner, on a particularly bright day, and there are those days: but anguish has your number, knows, to paraphrase the song, where you live. It's a difficult relationship, but mysteriously indispensable. It teaches you.

James Baldwin
quoted by W.J. Weatherby
James Baldwin: Artist on Fire

May 13   **Growth Through Pain**

<u>I celebrate my growth as I emerge from pain.</u>

I have developed sensitivity from my experience of being different and oppressed by my culture. I am thankful for what I have learned, in spite of the pain. Some people are hardened by their suffering or try to repress it, but I know it can also foster softness in me.

What can I do that will help me grow more sensitive instead of bitter? I need to acknowledge my pain and be honest about my feelings. If I deny the hurt, it will come out in destructive ways. My tears bring healing. I need to share what I am feeling with others and encourage others to come to me with their pain. The mutual support and understanding let me know that I am not alone and help me to see how similar my experiences are to those of others, despite different circumstances. I also need to give myself some time away from the problems of my life, finding joy in small pleasures and letting laughter bring its healing touch.

Today I use the memory of what I have experienced to heighten my awareness of other people's pain. I work for a more accepting world that does not inflict hurt on those who are lesbian and gay, and I affirm the special person I have become because of my same-sex orientation.

May 14 — Heroes

I remember asking the German reporter why I would be of interest to the German people...I said, "Other priests have AIDS," and he said, "Yes, but very few are willing to take the risks, not only of saying that they have AIDS, but that they are homosexual in the way you do with real assurance that you are loved by God and that everything is OK. That willingness to take those risks is what makes you news." Maybe what it takes to be a hero is to be willing to take the risk of being known for who you are and for telling the truth.

Father Robert L. Arpin
Wonderfully, Fearfully Made

May 15 — Heroes

<u>My heroes affirm the beauty of my loving.</u>

Do I need heroes? Someone on a pedestal doesn't really make *me* a better person. A celebrity who is lesbian or gay doesn't prove that *I* am a worthwhile person in my same-sex orientation.

At the same time, I need to know I am not alone. It helps me to know of famous lesbians and gay men to remind me that we truly are everywhere. With the assumption of heterosexuality all around me, I need openly lesbian and gay people to remind the world of its error.

Today I admire well-known people who are open about their same-sex orientation. I see their courage and feel courage within me. I see their goodness and sense that I am good also. They are not better than I am—I do not idolize them, but I see all of us as valuable human beings, worthy of respect, recognition and love.

As I value the lesbian and gay heroes in my life, I recognize myself as a hero as well. I have accomplished much in my life that is worthy of note, and that took courage. I have the makings within me of my own hero!

May 16 — Parenting

We are raising our son to see that our life is exceptional rather than unusual. We think this is an exceptional way to raise a child in any type of community, whether gay or straight.

Rob Sandoval and Bill Martin
quoted by Phillip Sherman and Samuel Bernstein
Uncommon Heroes

May 17   Parenting

<u>I am a competent, loving parent.</u>

    I see lesbian and gay parents being denied custody of their children over sexual-orientation issues. If I am a parent or want to have a child, I must reject the messages that I am unfit to parent because of my same-sex loving.

    My love for my child is clear, and I have special gifts to offer as a parent. My sexual orientation does not prevent me from being a wonderful parent. That I can love other adults in healthy ways enhances the loving atmosphere I provide for my child.

    When my child has problems related to my sexual orientation, I remember I am not to blame. The difficulty is homophobia, not who I am or whom I love. When the world accepts me as the healthy and normal person I am, sexual orientation will not be an issue for me or my child.

    I cannot control how my child responds, but I give my support and trust that the experiences I offer will lead my child into a healthy attitude about diversity and dealing with oppression. I provide a positive role model by staying true to myself and what I believe.

    Moving beyond my doubts about my parenting gives me more energy to focus on my relationship with my child. I embrace the wise and loving parent within me, as I confidently approach my child-rearing responsibilities.

May 18   Wholeness

*   Yes, Ann, I'm glad I'm gay. Thank you for asking. But being gay is a very small part of who I am. I'm a teacher and a football coach. I play classical music and a good game of tennis. I'm a gourmet cook. I can ski and I can sew. I am active in my church and a volunteer at our local shelter for the homeless. I don't believe in labels. Let's just say I am human.*

"From Louisville"
Ann Landers column

May 19   Wholeness

<u>I see my sexual orientation as part of a healthy totality.</u>

    I envision a world in which it is just as acceptable to be lesbian or gay as it is to be heterosexual. Living with societal oppression, I put a lot of energy into dealing with my sexual orientation in order to maintain my dignity. My challenge is to prevent that process from consuming me or detracting from the balanced person I want to be.

    My most important identity is as a human being. I explore what my personhood means for me and how I need to live that identity first and foremost. Every aspect of myself is vital—work, play, relationships, accomplishments, dreams, failures, communion

with the universe. All these areas deserve my energy.
Today I look at the totality of who I am. My sexual identity is a part, and I give it appropriate attention, but I also see my integrated self. I find joy in the wholeness of my experiences. As I triumph over unhealthy pressures, my multi-faceted self comes into focus.

May 20   Accomplishment

This has been a most wonderful evening. Gertrude has said things tonight it'll take her ten years to understand.
Alice B. Toklas
quoted by Amber Coverdale Sumrall
Write to the Heart

May 21   Accomplishment

<u>I am succeeding through my persistence.</u>

    I am growing and moving forward in all that I do. Sometimes when I experience failure, it feels like I'm not making progress, but I am learning from my mistakes. I realize my progress may not always be evident. As in learning to ride a bicycle, falling may feel like failure, but it actually is teaching me about maintaining my balance. Each apparent setback is bringing me closer to that revelatory moment of realizing that I have mastered an important life skill.
    When I face discrimination because of my same-sex loving, I remember that I am capable of succeeding under great odds. My life has been difficult, but I have survived. Looking at how much I have achieved, I know I can accomplish even more. I visualize success and am attaining it every minute.

May 22   Biblical Truths

As a Catholic who is also gay I gamble that the church has totally misinterpreted the Will and Word of God. If I am wrong then, the Church tells me, I will pay the price....Likewise, when the Church publicly condemns me and leads campaigns to eliminate my civil rights, they too gamble. If they are wrong (which I am sure they are), they will encounter a God who will greet them with "How in the hell could you do that to another human being?"
Brian McNaught
"Gay and Catholic"
Positively Gay

May 23   **Biblical Truths**

<u>I find truth in reinterpreted words.</u>

    Proudly I challenge the contentions of self-righteous people who use the Bible to "prove" I am evil and unnatural in my same-sex loving. If I was raised in a biblically-oriented religion, it may be difficult for me to reject such pronouncements. I know there are many parts of the Bible that do make sense to me. I can appreciate words of wisdom from the Bible without having to accept all of it, and I can reinterpret portions that were relevant in ancient times but need updating for a contemporary culture.

    I recognize the fallacy in taking passages out of context. The same books of the Bible that condemn same-sex love also claim it is sinful for women to wear red, have short hair, or speak out in church, while men are admonished not to wear wool and cotton at the same time or to have long hair.

    Instead I find biblical affirmation for same-sex loving in the bonds of David and Jonathan, or Ruth and Naomi. I remind myself of the purity of my loving in the biblical words, "there is nothing unclean of itself" (Romans 14:14). I find words in the Bible that speak to my heart, rejecting the half-truths and distortions. The goodness of my loving is revealed this very day through interpretations I find for myself! Amen!

May 24   **Integrity and Safety**

*   There is no reason why you should feel pressure to respond to a request for homosexual information any more than a brother or sister would feel called upon to respond to a request for detailed heterosexual information.*

                                                                                               Don Clark
                                                                       The New Loving Someone Gay

May 25   **Integrity and Safety**

<u>I balance my needs for integrity and safety.</u>

    Dealing with homophobic remarks in situations where I'm not out requires hard decisions. Do I come out in order to make a point? Do I try to take a stand without coming out? Or do I keep quiet to protect myself?

    I want to maintain integrity and personal safety at the same time, but that is not always possible. At times I realize my privacy is paramount and that the risk of coming out is not warranted. At other times I choose to come out to preserve my integrity and work against homophobia. There may also be times when I can speak out without declaring my sexual orientation.

    Deciding how to respond to homophobia often requires spur-of-the-moment judgments. I don't need to feel guilty if afterwards I wish I had responded differently. I made the best decision for myself at the moment. With each situation I gather more wisdom and courage for tomorrow as I respect what I need today.

May 26   **Creating Rituals**

You don't have to feel cheated because you can't have a wedding with organ music in the same church where your parents were married. Understand that heterosexual ceremonies and rituals around love are meant to reflect heterosexual erotic reality, not yours. If you yearn for ceremony, make your own...
                                                Emily L. Sisley and Bertha Harris
                                                             The Joy of Lesbian Sex

May 27   **Creating Rituals**

<u>I ritualize the special moments in my relationship.</u>
    I can be creative in finding ways to celebrate special times in my relationship. Married heterosexuals use the date of their wedding as their anniversary, and if I have a commitment ceremony or register as a domestic partnership, I have that anniversary, but I can find other special moments to memorialize as well. Is it when I first met my partner, our first date, the first time we were sexual with each other, when we moved in together? It could be when we first talked about love or commitment, when I took my partner to meet my family, or when we attended a special event together. I can have many anniversaries! In a culture that doesn't want to celebrate my love, I can celebrate it all the more myself.
    I am nurtured in my same-sex loving when I mark the milestones of my relationship. The acts can be simple or elaborate—a card or gift, a romantic date, a formal ritual, an exciting time of intimacy. My love is very important to me. I signify that importance by celebrating the memorable moments of our history together.

May 28   **Naturalness of Loving**

This is what I admire in other same-sex relationships that I can also claim for my own relationships: _____
_____
_____
_____

May 29   **Naturalness of Loving**

<u>Nature affirms the rightness of my loving.</u>
    It is a well-established scientific fact that homosexual activity occurs in many species, from bedbugs to the primates. Homosexual activity is as much a part of nature as sexuality itself. I celebrate the sexual rainbow shining in the firmament of nature.

Today I cast off pronouncements of perversion and sinfulness concerning my loving. Moving beyond shame, I let myself feel my attractions. I sense the naturalness of my sexuality in my lovemaking. In caring about my partner, I find the joy I know was intended for me.

As I delight in the beauty of my same-sex loving, I breathe in its goodness, and it fills my being. The harmony of nature affirms me, and so do I.

May 30   Grieving
Memorial Day

And if there is no ready answer, no logical explanation for the pain of those dying, for the fear of those who are ill, for the grief of those left behind—if there is no answer, there is for us assuredly a response.

We must love each other through this, for if compassion is not the most human of responses, then there is no hope. We must love each other through this, because all we have is each other.

John E. Fortunato
AIDS, the Spiritual Dilemma

<u>I learn about life from those who have died.</u>

This holiday emphasizes those who died in wars, but I also remember those who have died of AIDS. They too fought a brave battle. They too died with dignity. They too did not deserve to die.

When someone I care about has AIDS, I keep trying to find reasons why so many innocent people have been allowed to die. Today I quiet my questioning and accept that I have the strength to live in this complex universe without knowing all the answers. I need to have some sense of the meaning of life in order to find satisfaction in my daily living, but I also realize there are some things I may never be able to understand or explain.

I am ready to go on living, remembering those I loved so dearly and keeping them alive through my memories. On this day of remembrance, I honor those who have taught me the hard lessons of life through their deaths, as I use those lessons to grow in strength and wisdom.

May 31   **Sexual Ethic**

If we worship and serve our Creator instead of the creature, and experience life abundant, we can relate with each other as whole human beings—sexually, emotionally, and spiritually.

The Rev. Dan Geslin
"How Can Someone Be Both Christian and Homosexual?"
[unpublished paper]

June

June 1   **Sexual Ethic**

<u>I am respectful of myself and others in my sexuality.</u>

    I am a sexual being. Society has tried to suppress my sexual urges, but instead I celebrate them in all their glory. Today my challenge is to be responsible in how I satisfy myself sexually.

    What does it mean to be sexually responsible? My definition doesn't have to be the same as someone else's or what is considered "politically correct," but I know I need to be safe and I want to behave in a way that leaves me feeling good about myself. In learning what sexual behavior feels respectful of me and my partner, I follow my own higher self.

    When I feel strong attractions, I may be tempted to abandon my personal standard. I know I can control myself, though, and I remind myself to stop and listen to my inner voice before I act. My self-respect is more important than short-term sexual satisfaction. I make decisions that reflect love for myself and others.

June 2   **Homophobia**

*   I would like to draw a distinction between homophobia and homo-ignorance. There's much more homo-ignorance than there is homophobia, I think, and though it's difficult for us as a people, as a tribe, to hear the hate spewed at us, we know it's better for that hate to be public than for it to be secret.*

Paul Monette
The New York Times

June 3   **Homophobia**

<u>I rise above homophobia by seeking to understand it.</u>

    Homophobia is defined as the fear of homosexuality, but I often see anger or self-righteousness, not fear. I cope with bigoted people better when I remember the underlying fear they try to conceal. They may be struggling with a fear of part of themselves that is same-sex oriented. I know that fear.

    I think of my struggle with the homophobia inside myself. It has been easy to accept the negative stereotypes of lesbians and gay men. It has been easy to believe my culture's twisted logic. It has been difficult to face my same-sex attractions.

    I still find it challenging to communicate with those who try to intimidate me or treat me condescendingly, but deep within me I can at least partially understand. My attempts to understand aren't likely to change other people's behavior, but I am finding healing for myself. When the world refuses to understand me, I call forth my power of understanding. As I show it to others, I empower myself.

June 4 **Positive Imaging**

Every long journey begins with a dream,
A spirit with courage to make it all real;
The dream has been calling, been calling to you;
The dream is the only thing you want to do.

Ann Reed
"Expedition Song"
Just Can't Stop [audio recording]

June 5 **Positive Imaging**

<u>My dreams release new energy into the world.</u>

I have the right to dream. I won't let the difficulty of the struggle for my civil rights and acceptance of my sexual orientation make me settle for less than I deserve. When I feel hopeless, I remind myself that no one can take away my dreams. I nurture my capacity to envision the world I want for myself and others.

Today I imagine the person I long to be—perhaps in a different career, behaving differently in my relationships, doing what is really important to me. I see the "me" in my vision as no better than who I am right now, but as long as I am alive, I am changing, and I stretch myself by reaching toward the person in my mind.

I fantasize about the world in which I want to live—where I can walk safely after dark, where people smile at me when I kiss my lover in public, where my job is secure and being out at work is accepted. Beautiful pictures fill my mind and heart. As I and those who dream with me blend our positive energy, a new reality is emerging. I am dreaming a new world into being.

June 6 **Sexual Orientation**

I had a dream about not wanting to be straight. Margaret Thatcher decided that gays weren't doing society any good, so she got scientists to develop this gas...that would turn everybody straight. Now this leaked out onto the gay scene...and everybody bought gas masks. I was on Northampton Street when this gas bomb fell—there was green gas everywhere, and everybody on Northampton Street had a gas mask—everybody. But I woke up in a cold sweat, absolutely panicked, in case I didn't have one!

young lesbian
quoted by Melanie Chait
"Veronica 4 Rose"
[UK channel 4 television documentary]

June 7   **Sexual Orientation**

<u>I value the special gifts my same-sex loving brings me.</u>
    What would it mean to me to be heterosexual? Marriage would be a legal option for me. No more fear of gay-bashing! I could be "normal"!
    At the same time, I would lose the joy of my same-sex loving. There would be a whole new set of rules to play by. Would I become complacent, even oppressive of people who were different from me? What would happen to the sensitivity I have gained through my struggles?
    I am grateful for the special gifts that are mine in my same-sex orientation. I am free from the pressure to marry and have children. I have the chance to encounter a wide diversity of people. The opportunity for a truly equal relationship without one partner "owning" the other is a possibility. Not fitting the "norms," I can set my own rules in many areas of my life. I am being true to myself and am finding spiritual liberation in exploring that self. Taking on my same-sex orientation helps me let go of some unhealthy patterns in my culture and be open to change and new options. If I am out to friends and family, I have the gift of knowing who is willing to accept me unconditionally and support me.
    Today I realize how much I value the person I have become. I love myself just the way I am. I am at peace with myself and who I am today.

June 8   **Redefining Family**

    It's not just Mom, Dad and kids anymore—now family is who's there for you when you need them.
                                                                              William Finn
                                                                  on his play "Falsettos"
                                                                                People Magazine

June 9   **Redefining Family**

<u>I am creating a new family for myself.</u>
    My idea of family is more than biological bonds or a legal document. What does family mean to me? Is it someone who:
- accepts my same-sex loving without judgment?
- will support me years from now?
- is fun to be with?
- wants the same things I want?
- is willing to be involved with me financially?
- will get up in the middle of the night to help me?
- won't forget my birthday?

- feels safe when I need to cry?
- gives me advice and listens to mine?
- enjoys spending time with me?
- knows my faults and loves me anyway?

I will always be related to my family of origin, but I can also add new family to my life to fulfill needs that haven't been met. Thinking of people who fit my definition of family, I realize how special they are. I strengthen my connections with them and invite them into dialogue with me as we explore what our mutual nurturing means for each of us. My widening family circle enriches my life.

June 10 **Self-Liberation**

Wake up, you sleeping children.
Shake off your dreams and see,
The prisons are of our own making,
And the truth will set you free.

The Frontier is forever shifting...
Move on to the virgin lands.
Drink deep from the well,
For you never can tell,
The waters might turn into sand.
The waters might turn into sand.

Cris Williamson
"Frontier"
Live Dream [audio recording]

June 11 **Self-Liberation**

I cast off my bondage today.

What options do I have in my life? When I feel oppressed because of my same-sex orientation or have a hard time seeing the choices I have, I remember I can refuse to be a slave.

I consider alternatives in unsatisfactory areas of my life—job, school, home, friends, family, lovers, activities, obligations. Stretching my mind, I see the outrageous, the impractical, the scary, the silly. My thoughts expand, and some of the possibilities take on feasibility, even desirability.

As I explore my freedom, I also must ponder responsibility. When I relinquish my power to others, I am trying to escape responsibility for myself. I am ready to give up my bondage. Today I take control of my life. Freely I choose the direction for my future.

June 12 — Coming Out

If you are not afraid of the voices inside you, you will not fear the critics outside you.
Natalie Goldberg
Wild Mind

June 13 — Coming Out

As part of coming out, I am building self-love.

Before I come out to others, I need some level of self-acceptance for my same-sex orientation. With a lifetime of negative messages to counteract, I take my time. Today I dialogue with myself, honestly admitting my internalized homophobia. Without shaming myself, I own where I am and look at ways of developing more positive feelings. Gazing into the mirror, I tell myself how beautiful my love is. I write poetry to myself. With courage I reach out to others who support me in my loving. Books, music, and visual art can also affirm my same-sex orientation.

When is the time right for coming out? I ask my heart and have confidence in its reply. My first priority is building good feelings for myself; only then can I tell others who I am with pride.

June 14 — Risking Intimacy

Gay people can draw power from their strengths and learn how to handle their special problems. We do not need to be stuck in traditional heterosexual patterns of relationships and commitment. I believe that gay couples need to talk about and create new rules for love, rules that truly apply to homosexual relationships. This means not only relearning some rules that apply to any couple, but also discovering new rules that fit our own special needs. This is the dawning of a time to forge new paths and explore new ways for gay and lesbian couples to live and love.
Tina Tessina
Gay Relationships for Men and Women

June 15 — Risking Intimacy

I take the risk of intimacy in my relationships.

Am I ready to risk intimacy? When I fear rejection, I think of the joy of closeness. When my same-sex relationships seem insecure without legal and societal sanctions, I remind myself that I can still have commitment, if that is what I desire.

I look at how I have dealt with relationships in the past. Analyzing situations in which I have been able to achieve some level of intimacy, I consider how I can structure present and future relationships to allow for the closeness I desire. Can I set ground rules that help me feel safe enough to be open with other people? What support systems do I need in my relationship efforts?

I think about how I have had bonds with people that have endured without "official" ties of marriage or family. There are many different levels of commitment, and I decide what is meaningful for me.

Today I look at the gift of my same-sex orientation. Without stereotyped heterosexual male and female roles to hide behind, without a traditional marriage model to stagnate me, I am challenged to honest creative communication. I can acknowledge my fear while seeing the great potential for real intimacy. I want genuine relationships. They are worth the risk!

June 16   **Bond with the Oppressed**

Two days after I was elected, I got a phone call. The voice was quite young. It was from Altoona, Pennsylvania. The person said, "Thanks—you've made me believe in the Constitution of the United States for the first time ever."

So you see, you've got to keep electing gay people for that young child, and the millions upon millions like that child, to know there is hope for a better tomorrow. Not only for gays, but for blacks, Asians, the disabled, our senior citizens, and us!

Harvey Milk
quoted by Troy Perry and Thomas Swicegood
Profiles in Gay and Lesbian Courage

June 17   **Bond with the Oppressed**

I am one with the oppressed of the world.

When I think of myself as part of a minority group, I remember other groups that share a commonality with me. The oppression I have experienced because of my same-sex orientation creates a bond between me and many others in the world who have suffered—people of color, women, children and the aged, the poor and hungry in all countries, the differently abled, those who have been persecuted because of religious or class differences.

Although my specific experiences are different, the sense of being a member of an out-group is the same, and together we become the majority rather than the minority. As masses of humanity, we are bringing about change among the reluctant.

Even if I feel I am not suffering great discrimination at present, I keep sight of my dream for a just world. I am an outcast, but I am also an advocate. Together we make a difference in the world. I move forward with my sisters and brothers.

June 18 — Forgiveness

These are some of the people I may need to forgive because of the pain they have caused me:_____

_____

_____

June 19 — Forgiveness

<u>I heal myself as I forgive others.</u>

Making a response to the injustice I have experienced demands great strength from within my being. If those who hurt me asked for my forgiveness and admitted how they have wronged me, it might be easier, but such repentance is rare. Whether my pain is related to my same-sex loving or some other aspect of my life, I have been deeply hurt.

Today I look at those in my life I am being called on to forgive. Forgiveness is what I need to do for myself, not the offender. The offender is not absolved of responsibility for what was done, whether or not I forgive, and my forgiveness does not imply that what happened was acceptable. When I forgive, I let go of the hate in my heart, and that process cleanses my soul, allowing me to get on with my life. The chains of the offender's power over me are broken, and new health and purity grow within me.

I am ready to embark on a challenging and long journey. I love myself enough to do it. Let my self-healing forgiveness begin!

June 20 — Belonging
Summer Solstice

Each morning, I awake—a hundred men and a God.
We walk through the week's seven fingers
...into a thousand lives.

For we are one —
I am my sisters
And ye, my brothers

We thank the Universe to be alive;
We thank the Universe to be gay;
We thank the Universe to be me.

My life has become the Sabbath,
For I have touched the world
And I know that it is good.

...and this is just the beginning.

Bert Herrman
Being • Being Happy • Being Gay

June 21   **Belonging**
Summer Solstice

<u>I welcome summer blossoming into my life.</u>

    The freshness of the summer season calls out to me in rippling greens and rainbow flower petals. I put aside the sadness and hurt of my life and drink in the beauty. I am part of the beauty of the universe. Today I erase the messages from inside and out that try to tell me I am ugly or don't belong in the universe because of my same-sex orientation. My inner truth comes through clearly when I allow it. I am lovely and I am one with the universe. I free the smiles from their hiding places deep inside and let them out into the sun. I absorb the amazing blend of me and the unfolding summer. I am meant to be here right now, in the summer of my life.

June 22   **Richness of Identity**

I came to see gayness as a unique kind of mix of "ugly duckling" spiritual qualities. It creates, acts and dances. It bridges genders, races and classes, questions hetero "certainties," and has brought us through many holocausts.
                                                                  Jim Kepner
                                      "Mi Vida...Jim Kepner: Loner/Hero"
                                                           Square Peg

June 23   **Richness of Identity**

<u>My sexual orientation involves my whole being.</u>

    My same-sex attractions are a powerful part of my life. Whether in reality or fantasy, my sexual contacts are delicious and energizing, but they are not the whole of my life.

    My sexual identity is so much more than just sexual behavior. Today I reject a narrow definition of my life and paint a much larger picture of who I am. I look at same-gender issues in my thinking, my friendships, my view of the world, my political stances, my views of family and socialization, my life force, my spirituality, my visualization of a higher power. All these areas are affected by my sexual orientation. What I do in bed is only one of those images, and placing so much emphasis on my bedroom activity is neither healthy nor accurate.

    As I explore my whole being, I appreciate the way my same-sex loving weaves itself throughout. I am an intricate rainbow-colored mosaic—gay and glorious!

June 24 Nurturing Children

> We are all parents, every gay man and every lesbian, whether we have biological children or not. Our children are tomorrow's generations of gays and lesbians who are coming along. We have to give them roots. We have to sacrifice today, as all parents do, to give them a better world.
>
> Leonard Matlovich
> quoted by Troy Perry and Thomas Swicegood
> *Profiles in Gay and Lesbian Courage*

June 25 Nurturing Children

In nurturing children, I affirm my own inner child.

Whether I am a parent or not, I have connections with children. Every positive experience I have with a child brings hope to the world and vitality to my life. We shape the universe together.

In my same-sex orientation, I must fight society's messages about my relationships with children. I reject the condemning labels: child molester, unfit parent. Moving beyond society's false judgments of me, I develop healthy relationships with children.

It is time once again to close my ears to a blaming world and listen to the voice of truth inside me that names me a loving parent, a nurturer of children, one with both young and old in spirit. The nurturer in me reaches out to children with confidence and the child in me is fed by my communion with them.

June 26 Solidarity
Lesbian and Gay Pride March

> Our self love and our love for our gay sisters and brothers are the core of our revolution, and this love ultimately binds us together no matter what our exterior differences or opinions.
>
> Karla Jay
> *Out of the Closets*

June 27 Solidarity
Lesbian and Gay Pride March

I march in solidarity with those who share my pride.

Many years have passed since the first "Gay Power" rally that commemorated the Stonewall Inn riots. Accounts vary about what actually happened when police raided the Greenwich Village gay bar the night of June 27, 1969, but historians have documented the diversity of lesbians and gay men who participated in the several days of resistance. As I join with others to commemorate that symbol of the lesbian and gay political action movement, I celebrate the power we have in marching and working together.

With the amazing diversity among lesbians and gay men, it may seem at times that we are many communities rather than a unified group. But I have much in common with those who walk with me on this day of shared pride. When I find myself emphasizing our differences, I remind myself of our commonalities: our humaness, our same-sex orientation, our understanding of oppression, our need to belong to a larger community, our vision of liberation, and our pride in who we are as a people. When I am willing to look beyond how we are different to how we are similar, I find it easier to respect each person's journey and affirm that all of us are needed for our continued progress and liberation.

Today, I feel pride in what my community has accomplished over the years since Stonewall. Through our courage, our mutual empowerment, our tenaciousness, and our willingness to continue envisioning better tomorrows for ourselves and others, we have made a difference.

June 28 Facing Fear

People sometimes ask me, "Aren't you a little worried?...Aren't you afraid that someone will someday physically attack you or some of your followers?" Well, of course, that's on my mind....You know we have had to take that same stride down that lonely trail that our black brothers and sisters have been taking these past years. We have to go on even if they turn the vicious dogs loose upon us as they did on the blacks in Alabama, and in other places in the deep South. We have to go on and survive and push forward. You know that, once you wake up and know that you are an oppressed person.

Troy Perry
The Lord Is My Shepherd & He Knows I'm Gay

June 29 Facing Fear

I face my fear of gay bashing.

The possibility of being harmed because of my sexual orientation is real. Whether I have experienced overt abuse or not, I know it can happen to me. The threat of gay bashing makes me hesitant to be out in many situations. I feel especially vulnerable when I know I may not have protection from police or help from people around me.

My fear is valid, and it is natural to be afraid in the face of actual and potential threats. If my fear paralyzes me, though, I need to find some way of dealing with it that allows me to move on with my life. No one is ever safe in this world, but I can take reasonable precautions and then dare to be present in the world in spite of danger. Even in the midst of an insane world, I can act sanely. In my quest for a full life, I decide what risks I am willing to take. Living in constant fear is not being fully alive. Censoring my

every move is not being fully alive. At the same time, taking careless risks is inviting trouble.
    Today I face my fears. I make wise decisions around the threats of gay bashing. Being truly alive is my challenge. I accept it with courage.

June 30　　　　　　　　　　　　　　　　　　　　　　　　**Contrasts Within**

Like drops of water that can wear away the rock, the small can use intelligence, persistence, and will to defend themselves—like a peasant nation against an imperialist war machine.

Holly Near
album jacket
Watch Out [audio recording]

July

July 1　　　　　　　　　　　　　　　　　　　　　　　　**Contrasts Within**

<u>I love both the strong and the gentle within me.</u>

    When I look at who I really am, I see both strength and gentleness. I am able to move beyond the stereotypes of the macho straight man, the meek straight woman, the "butch" lesbian, and the effeminate gay man. I appreciate the range of traits within each of us.
    As my self-love grows, I see the miracle of my strength and gentleness intertwining, just as they combine in nature despite seeming contradictions. The mountain stream that looks so harmless cuts deep crevices in the rocks. Small plants bent over by the wind are able to force their way through pavement. A tiny seed grows into a towering tree.
    Today I embrace the opposites within me as totally compatible. I am powerful and weak, masculine and feminine, dominant and submissive. I am more complex than a single word or trait, and I treasure all the diversity integrated into my wonderful self.

July 2　　　　　　　　　　　　　　　　　　　　　　　　　　　**Love Ethic**

There is a depth to our struggle that is hard to grasp. It is above all else a struggle for the freedom to love; it is a struggle to break free from all the obstacles to love and intimacy. This victory will be not just for gay people, but for the entire human community.

John J. McNeill
Taking a Chance on God

July 3 — Love Ethic

<u>My ethical decisions reflect what is most loving.</u>

The rules I grew up with don't fit my life today. I need to decide what is right and wrong on my own. In my same-sex loving, I am finding ways of being with people that are different from what I was taught to expect. My moral and ethical code is one more area where I must be creative.

Today I choose a single rule for myself—living by what is most loving. Evaluating each situation, I base my decision on love: love for myself, love for others, love for the earth. The decisions aren't easy—having a prescribed set of guidelines would be much simpler—but I know other people's rules don't work for me. I trust myself and my ability to make wise decisions. I believe in the power of love to work good in the world. My ethics direct me along a clear path of compassion. My life is given over to love.

July 4 — Freedom
Independence Day

We marched in 1963 with Dr. Martin Luther King, and we dared to dream that freedom would include us. Because not one of us is free to choose the terms of our living until all of us are free to choose.

Audre Lorde
1983 Civil Rights March
Washington, D.C.

<u>I continue to affirm the ideal of freedom as I deal with hypocrisy.</u>

On this holiday that celebrates freedom in my country, I look beyond areas in which freedom has not been achieved and work toward what I know is possible. I won't ignore the hypocrisy of a nation that claims to stand for freedom but allows blatant discrimination and oppression of many minorities, including lesbians and gay men. At the same time I keep alive the dream that one day everyone, including me, will be free.

How do I live in a culture of hypocrites without becoming so cynical that I am poisoned by it? How do I find energy to keep fighting for what I know is right? How do I find the courage to stand up for what I believe?

I am making a difference in this world by being who I am. My efforts may seem small, but they join with those of all freedom-fighters past, present and future to create a force that changes the world. Countless souls have been part of the struggle, and each day we are moving closer to our goal. Taking heart in the progress that has been made, I hold close the vision of freedom and plan how I will be part of it. I celebrate this holiday of liberation.

July 5 — Being Single

I have had my last insane relationship. No joke. Really. I've had every kind of insane relationship there is to have, and now, before I get together with a mass murderer or something, I think I will try being celibate for a while and see how it goes. Who knows? It could be wonderful.

unnamed lesbian
quoted by JoAnn Loulan
Lesbian Passion

July 6 — Being Single

I find satisfaction in being alone.

It's all right to want to be in a relationship, but when that is not happening for me, I need to find ways of having a fulfilling life by myself and not become desperate about finding a new partner.

Today I remind myself that I am a whole person whether I am in or out of a relationship with a lover. My life can be a wonderful adventure just as it is, and I am finding out much about myself in this time of being single. Friends and family give me support and closeness. My work and hobbies bring me a sense of purpose and fun.

I explore the difference between being alone and being lonely. I take time to nurture myself and get to know myself, exploring the many aspects of self-intimacy—emotional, spiritual, and sexual. I learn to appreciate my strength and self-sufficiency.

I consider whether there are parts of myself I denied when I was in a relationship that I can now develop. Did I give up hobbies because my partner did not share them? Did I change my living-space to something I didn't like because of my partner's preferences? This is my time to reclaim what is important to me.

I am careful not to isolate myself because of not being part of a couple. This is a time to be with the important people in my life. I consider new interest groups and seek out situations in which I can feel comfortable with other single people, but I also let myself be with couples and realize I can have meaningful interaction with them as an individual.

I live in the here and now, not always hoping for something different. Tomorrow will come on its own without my trying to orchestrate it. I see the beauty in my life today and trust that the beauty will continue regardless of the direction my life takes. I savor the goodness of this alone time in my life.

July 7 — Growing Old

Here is what is positive for me about getting older: _____

_____

_____

_____

July 8 — Growing Old

<u>I appreciate the benefits of getting older.</u>

In some cultures older people are honored for their wisdom and given high status. Living as I do in an ageist culture where youth is glorified, I must create the honor for my aging self without the outside affirmation I deserve. In addition, I have the challenge my sexual orientation presents as I grow older—fewer social sanctions and legal protections that provide support in old age, such as traditions around relationships with "in-laws," and partners' Social Security or pension benefits.

Today I look beyond my apprehension and focus on the blessings of aging. I have learned much from my years of living, both in the challenges I have met through my same-sex loving and in other aspects of my life. My time of retirement offers new freedom in its reduced responsibilities and added leisure time. As I increasingly come to terms with life, I am finding a greater serenity. The skills for living learned in my youth serve me well. I treasure enduring connections with people who stand with me through hard times. My heart is peaceful, and I anticipate the later years of my life as truly golden.

July 9 — Individuality

The word is out. "You are perfect." Each of us has the potential within us to be one perfect example of ourself. We are each a unique creation, as different as every snowflake. Your combination of chromosomes never existed before anywhere. As an acorn is meant to become an oak tree, you are meant to become you.

Bert Herrman
Being • Being Happy • Being Gay

July 10 — Individuality

<u>I treasure my uniqueness.</u>

In loving someone of my own gender, I consider similarities and differences between myself and others. Although I feel strong bonds with those of the same sex, I remind myself that I am different from every other person, regardless of gender.

I explore ways in which I differ from my lovers, my lesbian and gay friends, and well-known people who are openly lesbian or gay. I resist the desire to try and imitate others in order to be more acceptable to them or avoid conflict with those I care about. I respect others' right to be who they are, while at the same time affirming my own beauty that sets me apart from every other person on earth.

Commonality strengthens relationships, but differences enrich them. When I celebrate my uniqueness, I share the freshness of my being with those around me and increase my love for myself. Even if I am rejected for who I am, my gifts mean no less just because they are not joyfully welcomed.

I am making a difference. My individuality is part of the splendor of the universe.

July 11 **Embracing Anger**

Sharon, I feel the pain of our separation every day. Since I couldn't be with you, I had to do something with my rage or it would have destroyed me. I decided to speak out and work for a positive change to come out of all you and I have suffered.
                                                                Karen Thompson
                                                                Why Can't Sharon Kowalski Come Home?

July 12 **Embracing Anger**

I use anger as a positive force.

I visualize anger as molten glass being worked by the skilled glass blower. If it is too hot, it becomes too difficult to mold and cannot be controlled. If it cools too quickly, however, it cracks, and the beauty of the piece is lost. When it is the proper temperature, something special is created.

Living in a society that tells me my anger is bad, I remind myself that anger can be constructive or destructive. When I let my anger become too hot, I lose control and am ineffective, perhaps even violent. When I try to stay cool, the anger may turn inward against me, or sideways in non-productive actions. Channeling energy from the rage I feel towards the world's condemnation of my sexual orientation, I can accomplish good if I use my fury well. Indignation mobilizes me to fight for what I need personally, as well as to work for peace and justice in the world. When I deal with anger promptly and productively, it increases my momentum.

Today I embrace my anger. I value the forward motion it provides. I use its energy to change my life for the better.

July 13 **Choosing Community**

We provided each other with a context to understand ourselves as part of a greater whole. This is a fluid relationship, not a fixed one. We are at once, generation to generation, each other's future and past. Disconnected from each other, we...are held prisoners of heterosexual society's perception of us. We are unable to shape our own community and individual identities. But aware of our past and intergenerationally connected we can better interpret and understand ourselves in the present—and we can better shape for ourselves and those who follow a more secure future.
                                                                Marcy Adelman
                                                                Long Time Passing

July 14 — Choosing Community

<u>I choose connections with people thoughtfully.</u>

Gay bars and social clubs, along with support groups and religious organizations for lesbians and gay men, address my needs, but they emphasize my isolation from the mainstream culture. My longterm vision is to be fully accepted and integrated into society, but in the reality of today's world, I sometimes need the empathy of lesbian and gay groups for my sense of well-being.

Only I can decide what situations are right for me. I find settings that nurture and foster my self-love, whether they are exclusively same-sex oriented or inclusive of others. I may become involved in less secure environments for various reasons —political, economic, or whatever—but I give priority to what is best for me. I don't need to feel apologetic about choosing to be with other lesbians and gay men. I need those connections for support, for perspective, and for the community effort that will bring about change in society as a whole.

In my dreaming, I hold the image of an all-affirming, non-oppressive humanity, but for now I find loving places to grow in the present, while trusting that my choices make the possibility of wider options for tomorrow more likely.

July 15 — Spectrum of Life

We carry so much power in our hearts, we gay people. We carry so much beauty and so much untapped love. It is time for us to blossom, time for us to remember who we are, and rejoice in it. We are a part of the world, and the world needs us, even if it does not think so. We are everyone's children, lovers, teachers.

Andrew Ramer
Two Flutes Playing

July 16 — Spectrum of Life

<u>I celebrate the rainbow in myself and the world.</u>

The full spectrum of life calls to me. No longer do I see myself in "either-or" terms. I love *and* hate; I teach *and* learn; I am a healer *and* one who is being healed; I am part of humanity yet ever alone; I change while staying the same; I am living and dying all at once.

My recognition of the range within myself helps me also to see others as parts of the continuum. I don't need others to be at the same place I am—my own position shifts, as everyone's does. In this fluid diversity is the beauty of the rainbow. It colors the world and challenges my efforts to harmonize.

Respecting who I am, I look forward today to where I will be tomorrow and honor where I have been in the past. In my same-sex orientation, I expand the possibilities for love. My being weaves sparkling threads into the wonderment of the universe.

July 17   **Choosing Friends**

I had the Quixotic notion that I could continue to enjoy all kinds of society, the bohemian and the elite, the straight and the gay. I know many persons in "the gay world" who accomplish this trick with apparent ease...In any case I was too bizarre in my behavior, during this decade, for even the conservative members of the gay world.

Tennessee Williams
Memoirs

July 18   **Choosing Friends**

I choose my friends wisely.

Thinking about who my friends are gives me clues about myself. If most of my friends are straight, am I denying my same-sex orientation? If most of my friends are lesbian and gay, am I becoming more isolated from the world at large than I want to be? I consider what the mix of straight, bisexual, lesbian and gay people in my life says about the choices I am making.

Sometimes I need more lesbian and gay friends to affirm my sexual orientation, to give me a sense of community, or to provide a feeling of safety. At other times, I need more contact with straight friends to help me realize my part in the larger world community. My bisexual friends experience discrimination as I do, but can give me a different perspective on sexual orientation issues.

I look at the people I choose to spend time with, exploring the reasons for my choices. Finding relationships helpful to my sense of well-being creates a healthful place for myself in the world. My decisions regarding friendships help me learn and grow.

July 19   **Coming Out**

We can come into our power as lovers by coming out. There is great power in naming ourselves. For you to come out will contribute to the well-being of us all insofar as you are participating in shaping the Sacred among us.

Carter Heyward
Touching Our Strength

July 20   **Coming Out**

I affirm the rightness of my loving.

When I come out to another person without apology, I am proclaiming that my same-sex love is honorable. If I hide in a closet, even for self-protection, I do so at a cost.

I know my loving is a natural part of the universe. In situations that feel right, I assert to others my pride in this part of who I am. Even if my words are shunned, my act of telling has an impact on both myself and others.

It takes time for the world to truly hear my words in concert with millions of others, but little by little my message is changing attitudes and actions. As I speak my truth to others, I also affirm it for myself. Today I listen to my reality and accept my goodness. My loving is lovely.

July 21 — Naming My Abuse

We conceived of this collection out of our own sense of the empowering force of writing out of our worst feelings and fantasies. Bringing them out of the shadows began to get them to a manageable size. If a poem or scene could be shaped from the garbage heap of our memories, our bodies and psyches could begin to heal themselves.

Toni McNaron and Yarrow Morgan
Voices in the Night

July 22 — Naming My Abuse

<u>I accept my perceptions of the abuse I have experienced.</u>

I am ready to name the abuse I have suffered. Whether I have experienced sexual, physical, emotional or spiritual abuse, the hurt is real. I see others whose mistreatment seems more severe, but I won't discount what happened to me. All abuse is damaging. If the violation was less overt, such as with emotional abuse, I tend to deny its importance or even the fact that it actually happened. However, I need to trust what my inner voice tells me. Believing that my perceptions are valid is the first step in my healing process.

Writing the words that tell about my abuse emphasizes the reality for me, and as I build trust in myself, I am gathering the courage to share my story with others. Letting others read what I have written or saying the words out loud can be frightening, but it is an important part of the naming and healing.

Today I acknowledge what has happened to me. My willingness to confront and name this truth is bringing me to a healthier, happier self. I am learning to trust and share my reality.

July 23 — Sexual Orientation

I do not want to get stuck in the why's of who I am...nor do I want you to. Be it genetic or learned behavior for whatever set of reasons or circumstances, I am who I am. There is no fault or blame. It simply is. And the most important consideration is acceptance and dealing with that truth.

Bud
quoted by Rob Eichberg
Coming Out: An Act of Love

July 24   **Sexual Orientation**

<u>My sexual orientation is right for me whether I choose it or am born with it.</u>

    The debate goes on. Is everyone born with the capacity to respond sexually to both genders and the freedom to choose heterosexuality, homosexuality, or bisexuality? Or was my sexual orientation unalterably set by the time of my birth? Those who claim my sexual orientation is acceptable only if it is proven inborn, can always find ways of discounting that information, just as racists always find rationalizations for discriminating against people of color.
    It really doesn't matter whether I choose my orientation or not. I feel within me the rightness of who I am.
    I see my sexual orientation as the gift it is. Whether I choose or am chosen, I am fine just the way I am. I let myself be exactly who I am without explanation.

July 25   **Self-Acceptance**

*   I want to explore some of the talents I've discovered that I have. Everybody always thought I had it all together. Now, I believe in more of my talents than I did before.*
                                                        Barbee J. Cassingham and Sally M. O'Neill
                                                                                And Then I Met This Woman

July 26   **Self-Acceptance**

<u>I free myself to grow by letting me be who I am.</u>

    It is a seeming contradiction that sometimes I have to accept myself as I am before I am free to change. If my energy goes into resisting parts of me, how can I find the energy to grow? I can worry about making changes some other time. For now, I relinquish my self-criticisms and comparisons with other people.
    I am ready to embrace who I am. In a disapproving world, I must look hard for acceptance, and much of it needs to be generated from within myself.
    I let the beauty of my same-sex loving dispel my doubts. As I see parts of myself I can love easily, I become conscious of other wonderful aspects within me. My radiance expands before me. I visualize my self-love encircling my being and wrapping me in the warmth of its protective shield.

July 27   **Separateness**

I look forward to the future because I believe that as Ray's and my relationship grows more mature, I will learn to confidently celebrate my individuality....When Ray and I first got together, we described relationship as a means of enabling each other to grow to our full potential. Somewhere along the line, like most everyone else, we lost sight of our goal and began to function as one entity. Mature love encourages individual growth in the presence of one who is patient, forgiving and supportive.

Brian McNaught
A Disturbed Peace

July 28   **Separateness**

<u>I maintain my sense of self in my relationships.</u>

In a culture that refers to marriage relationships as "two becoming one," the dominant model for a close relationship is fusion. Having been pressured to be someone different from my natural self, I appreciate how important it is to retain my individual identity in or out of relationships. I reject the self-effacing image of two half-beings merging into some vague wholeness.

I don't need another person for completion of myself. If I give up who I am for my partner, the relationship will be empty. My personhood apart from my significant other brings a richness to our interactions, and becoming carbon copies of each other is not the solution to working out differences.

In my same-sex orientation, I have more freedom to discard the "straight-jacket" of fusion. I am a pioneer in my loving as I celebrate the totality of me!

July 29   **Change**

There were those who worked very hard in the church, but who wanted us all to go slow, to take a very conservative posture in our approach to any social reforms. They felt, in all honesty, that political action, demonstrations, fasts, and marches were premature. I didn't agree then; I still don't. But I respect their opinions....I felt that the spectrum of the church's outreach was such that it would accommodate all. It does!

Troy Perry
The Lord Is My Shepherd and He Knows I'm Gay

July 30   **Change**

<u>I find my own ways of working for change in the world.</u>

How am I changing the world? I am having an impact just by being myself and living authentically from day to day, but I can also be intentional in working for change. In my same-sex orientation, I desire sweeping transformation in this homophobic, unjust world. I want to have a part in bringing about these changes.

Dealing with others on a one-to-one basis can have far-reaching effects—coming out forces people to deal with sexual orientation issues; confronting people on homophobic remarks raises their awareness; explaining my reality helps others understand.

Political action can also bring about progress—demonstrating, writing to legislators, joining and supporting organizations that work for social justice. I can work in overt or subtle ways.

At times the tactics of some may seem extreme, even counterproductive, but how can I know what will ultimately bring about meaningful change? I respect the right of others to choose their way of being in the world. Different approaches may be effective in varying situations or at different times. I know I don't have all the answers. Choosing my own methods, I let others find theirs. I join with the changers and movers in shaping tomorrow.

July 31   Living with AIDS

When the normal response was to react with fear and panic, there were people dancing backward, responding with love and confidence. When, every day, the world began repeating a death mantra, our sacred clowns danced the dance of life. They talked about living with AIDS, surviving, healing, recovering. When the normal reaction to a diagnosis was isolation, [they] dragged us into a community. When the world wanted us to be victims, they drew circles of light around themselves and stood in their power.

Perry Tilleraas
The Color of Light

August

August 1   Living with AIDS

I learn and I teach about healing as I deal with AIDS.

I affirm that we all are living with AIDS because it exists, and because we can never see the world in the same light now that it moves among us. Even those who believe they don't know anyone with AIDS are touched by their knowledge of its existence.

People of same-sex orientation are responding to AIDS with a breadth of love and hope beyond imagination. I am proud to be part of this compassionate community and am learning to see wholeness in all people, beyond our diseases of body or soul. As I reach out to others in love, I experience healing flowing to and from my own being.

Our proclamation is that we heal through life and through death. We are creating a new definition of healing that reaches into our depths and extends beyond our lifetimes.

My life is a lesson that speaks too loudly to be ignored. I am a healer as I find healing for myself in the reality of a world living with AIDS.

August 2   **Sense of Commonality**

Being a swimmer who's an out gay man means that I have more than water to buoy me up.

                                        Bruce Hayes, Olympic gold medal swimmer
                                                 quoted by Phillip Sherman and Samuel Bernstein
                                                                                 Uncommon Heroes

August 3   **Sense of Commonality**

<u>I appreciate the community of others who are out.</u>

    When my community seems small and I feel isolated by my same-sex orientation, I search for the evidence that "we are everywhere." I look for openly lesbian and gay people in the performing arts, in politics, in the media. They remind me that lesbians and gay men can be out in many circumstances. I learn from them about being true to myself and reaching for my dreams. They are my role models of courage. I don't have to imitate them unless I choose to, but I am in solidarity with them. Together we are making our mark in the world—they in their way, I in mine.

    Knowing I am not alone brings an enduring serenity to my being. My view of my community expands, starting with where I live and radiating outward. I take my place in a worldwide network of special loving people.

August 4   **Inner Child**

If I could go back through time and speak to myself as a child, this is what I would say:

_____

_____

_____

_____

August 5   **Inner Child**

<u>I nurture the child within me.</u>

    Remembering my early years, I see the part of my child who was never affirmed for being different. I grieve the invisibility of others like me and recall the struggle to be who I am. Letting myself go back, I get in touch with all the parts of that child left hurting, all the holes in the nurturing I experienced.

Today I find ways of parenting myself. Reaching inside to my sad and frightened child, I blanket that being in love. I celebrate my child for all that was and is and will be. Whatever my age, my child lives on and longs for the healing touch that comes from within and flows back to my inner spirit.

I find ways of giving my child expression. The wide-eyed toddler spellbound by holiday lights, the silly kindergartner giggling at nothing, the giddy teenager falling in love—they continue to live within my being and hunger for the chance to laugh. As a mature adult I can still affirm that child.

I rejoice at the blending of adult and child within me. Every part of me needs love, every part of me is lovable. As I love the child within me, I am freeing my adult to grow. My child is healing my life.

August 6   **Commitment Ceremony**

Rituals do have power. It's very powerful to have a ritual where a community of people acknowledge and celebrate a relationship.

Jeffrey Friedman
quoted by Phillip Sherman and Samuel Bernstein
Uncommon Heroes

August 7   **Commitment Ceremony**

<u>I create my own definition of commitment and how to celebrate it.</u>

I ponder the significance of having a commitment ceremony whether or not I choose to have one. I don't need a ceremony to legitimize what I share with a lover. My love is a natural part of the universe, but a ritual can proclaim that legitimacy, affirm our time together, make a pledge for the future, elicit the support of friends and family, or invoke a blessing upon the union. Growing up with the expectation of marriage, I may desire that tradition as a fulfillment of a dream.

Today I reject unhealthy expectations for a committed relationship. Living in a culture that acknowledges a high divorce rate while still encouraging "death-do-us-part" pledges has given me confusing messages. I find ways of being positive about my relationship without being unrealistic. I develop a definition of commitment that makes sense for my life while clarifying the energy I bring to sustaining a relationship. I have gifts to offer in a relationship, and one of them is a thoughtfulness regarding healthy commitment.

August 8   **Coming Out**

So I finally decided that I was gay, like in the seventh grade.
But I didn't tell anybody yet because I figured it was just a phase. That's what they tell you. So I decided to wait a year, and if I was still gay in a year, I would tell my parents...
   And then, like, a year later I was all set to tell my family. I decided that it wasn't a phase, I was gay...And then I decided to wait until National Coming Out Day, which was when everybody was supposed to tell everybody that they're gay. I was all set to do it and I chickened out again. ...
   So finally...We were eating dinner. My sister said, "Boy, Erin sure is hungry, isn't she?"
   And I said, "Yeah. And I'm gay too."

Erin
quoted by Kurt Chandler
"Growing Up Gay"
Star Tribune, Minneapolis-St. Paul

August 9   **Coming Out**

<u>I set my own timetable for coming out.</u>

So many pressures and opportunities to come out—Gay Pride marches, National Coming Out Day, probing questions from others, political causes needing advocacy.

If I am outed, I have no choice, but at other times, coming out is my personal decision, and I choose what is right for me. I may decide a moment is right, even if I have not planned for it; I look at my needs, my readiness, my timing. When the situation doesn't feel right for me, I refuse to yield to pressure.

Today I respect my own process. Although I am part of a world community, I must set the direction for my life. I have my own coming-out day, and it is on the calendar of my conscience.

August 10   **Accepting Love**

Wholeheartedly invite new people into your life. Nature abhors a vacuum. While you are free to grow alone, you are also free to find the one looking for you.

Celeste West
A Lesbian Love Advisor

August 11   **Accepting Love**

<u>I deserve to be loved, by me as well as others.</u>

    When I am hesitant to risk intimacy with another person, I consider if my reluctance is related to a lack of self-esteem. Am I rejecting someone's love for me because I don't love myself enough? I must value myself so as not to mistrust someone who admires me.

    I start by acknowledging the beauty of my gender. The beauty I am attracted to in others exists in myself. I look further at who I am, at my distinctive qualities. I appreciate that I am worthy of love—my love and others' love.

    As I look in the mirror at the radiance shining back, I see someone who is valued by others. I get in touch with the love I experience from others. That love is real. That love is deserved. I celebrate all the love in my life—love I give to myself and others, love flowing to me from caring people and from the universe.

August 12   **Lovemaking**

    Somewhere between our second and third date, it comes to me in a flash. There is nothing second-rate about this. *I am on Cloud Nine, feeling every kind of attraction all at once, I want to give to him in the worst way...this is love and it's great. I write it down to make it official. With these plain words I take my life into my arms: I accept my gayness. It is my way of loving.*

                                                                                                    Gary J. Stern
                                                                      A Few Tricks Along the Way

August 13   **Lovemaking**

<u>I celebrate the naturalness of my lovemaking.</u>

    Today I banish the hurtful words, looks, and actions of the outside world from my bedroom. As I approach my lover, I exclude any phantom intruders. Our time together is for us alone, and I claim this delight in full. When I behave responsibly with my sexuality, I am loving myself as well as my lover, and I feel pride in my same-sex loving.

    As my lover and I open ourselves to each other, I let the naturalness of our intimacy sweep over me. My body is sensitive to our pleasuring touch. My senses are heightened, and I bring my whole being into this joyful experience. Our time of loving is a celebration of the person I am meant to be.

August 14 — Positive Action

I've been waiting for this for 20 years. Not just waiting around but working and hoping and praying. It just touches me very deeply.

Karen Clark, legislator
on the passage of the 1993 Minnesota gay rights legislation
Star Tribune, Minneapolis-St. Paul

August 15 — Positive Action

<u>I find positive ways of working for change.</u>

When I resist systems or people, I give them energy and drain myself. In issues regarding my same-sex orientation, it is especially challenging to find ways of being constructive as I work for change.

I remember today that working for a cause is more effective than working against one. As I think of my vision for the world, I frame my desires in positive terms. In my personal life as well as with my political stances, I devise ways of being pro-active. I stand in community with all who are building rather than tearing down.

Change is happening all around me, and I am part of the process. My positive efforts are having an impact on both my life and the progress of humanity.

August 16 — Unconditional Love

In a context of love we allow ourselves and others to experience all there is. A context of love is enormous, powerful, and healing. It is large enough to include sadness, pain, disappointment, hurt, anger, confusion, guilt, aimlessness, anxiety, joy, exhilaration, ecstasy, and the truth. When we love ourselves and others we have lots of room to experience the process of coming out and the process of life. Love is not based on right or wrong, good or bad. Deep in the center of our being we know that when we love someone, we love them no matter what.

Rob Eichberg
Coming Out—An Act of Love

August 17 — Unconditional Love

<u>I surround myself with people who give me unconditional love.</u>

I need people in my life who like *all* of who I am, including my sexual orientation. I challenge the fallacy of those who claim to love me but hate my sexual orientation, which is an integral part of my being. Realizing I deserve unconditional love, I don't

need to settle for anything less.
When people try to change me in ways that are disrespectful, I turn away. I seek out people and groups that accept me for who I am. Severing relationships is painful, but I have the courage to choose what is right for me. If I surround myself with judgmental people, I cannot give myself the total acceptance I need.
I bring affirming people into my life. I am giving myself unconditional love by asking no less from others.

August 18 **Lesbian and Gay Pride**

Valuing our personal experience contributes to our belief in self-worth. A healthy pride results. The current political and spiritual movement of gay and lesbian pride expresses our recovery of a sense of awe at our experience and a valuing of it. I say "current," because there have been other gay and lesbian pride movements throughout history, most recently in Germany prior to the Nazi rise to power. That the movement was destroyed and a quarter of a million of us were murdered in concentration camps serves as a sobering reminder of the ebb and flow of our acceptance. Some who participated in those murders were themselves homosexuals who did not enjoy a sense of self-worth—all the more reason for us to share our sense of pride with others.

Chris Glaser
Coming Home

August 19 **Lesbian and Gay Pride**

<u>I take the triangle as a symbol of pride.</u>

In Nazi concentration camps, the pink triangle was used to identify gay men and the black triangle, lesbians. They were symbols of condemnation and instruments of inhuman oppression. Why would I want to adopt symbols forced upon my sisters and brothers in the Holocaust?

As I think about the pink and black triangles, I realize they are part of my history. The Nazi oppression, and all oppression of lesbians and gay men, are real and do not go away by not thinking about them. Many historical accounts ignore this part of history, but I fight the invisibility that has been so common. I embrace the pink and black triangle as I claim them for myself.

The Nazis meant the triangles to be symbols of shame, but I use them as symbols of pride. I wear them as a message to others that I am willing to be who I am. I can wear them with the point down as the Nazis used them, to preserve authenticity, or pointing upward, as a sign of communion with my higher power.

Today I take the pink and black triangles in solidarity with lesbians and gay men everywhere, and use them as signs of hope for a non-oppressive world.

August 20   **Trustworthy Voices**

The other voice that speaks to us from our inner dialogue is the voice of limitless love. It is the voice that speaks to us of possibility. Possibility creates feelings of joy. Whenever we have acted on a hunch and had that hunch come through, it was this voice which spoke to us. Or when we aimed for a goal and knew in our heart we could achieve it, it was this voice which told us it was so.

George Melton
Beyond AIDS

August 21   **Trustworthy Voices**

<u>I choose sources of guidance carefully.</u>

    As a child I was told that others knew what was best for me. Now that I am an adult, I realize I have the wisdom and judgment to know what I need. Because of my same-sex orientation, I must be careful which voices I listen to—many try to dissuade me from the path that is right for me.

    I choose my outside voices carefully: friends, therapist, spiritual guide, doctor. I seek their wisdom, but I evaluate their words for the truth they give to my life, and when that truth does not fit me, I find other sources of knowledge and inspiration.

    The voice I need most to hear is my own. I need to reach deeply within myself to avoid the negative messages from outside that have been instilled in me, and discover my real truth. I listen to the positive words from within myself. Bringing their light to the surface, I let their brightness fill my being. My voices of truth lead me forward.

August 22   **Coming Out to Family**

Here are the gifts I see for myself in being out to my family:_____

_____

_____

By coming out to my family, I give them these gifts, whether they appreciate them or not: _____

_____

_____

August 23   **Coming Out to Family**

<u>I approach coming out to family with thoughtfulness and courage.</u>

    Coming out to family is seldom easy. Although I think I know them well, I cannot predict how they will react to learning about my same-sex orientation. I know I have much to gain and much to lose, depending on the outcome.

My first priority must be what is important for me. Yet, it is also important to think about what it will mean to my family members—possible hurt, disappointment, shock, denial, a sense of loss—probably the same feelings I experienced as I came out to myself. My disclosure is likely to cause some pain, but I remind myself that the pain is not my fault—it is a result of homophobia. I also remember that by coming out I am creating the possibility of more honest and intimate relationships. That possibility will enrich my family, if they communicate openly with me.

Although being out changes relationships, I am still the same person I was before my revelation. I give others time to grow with this new knowledge, as I continue to be gentle with myself. Although I cannot control how others relate to me, I am dealing with my life in an honest and courageous way.

August 24   **Commonality Through Pain**

I don't think it's any easier to become a homosexual, with the permissiveness that we're developing these days, than it is to become a heterosexual. It's not easy to become a human being.

Marty Rockland
quoted by Dale Beldin and Mark Krenzien
Who Happen to Be Gay [video]

August 25   **Commonality Through Pain**

<u>I am bonded with humanity through the struggles of life.</u>

When I feel alone in my pain, I remember that all human beings experience difficult times. My same-sex loving brings particular problems, but the emotions I feel are common to all people. Loss causes grief, whether the loss is of a loved one, a business or a piece of heirloom jewelry. Injustice causes pain, whether the injustice arises from discrimination, loss of innocent lives or family favoritism. Struggling with dishonesty can involve coming-out decisions, co-workers who steal, or cheating on a test.

Sensing the pain of the world does not diminish my personal agony, but it creates a bond with others. When I realize the universality of my experiences, it is easier to seek support, search for answers, and move beyond my problems into serenity. I acknowledge the reality of my struggles without shame and continue my life journey as part of the human community, reaching for the light in concert with others.

August 26   **Stereotypes**

Male and female created He me.

Quentin Crisp
The Naked Civil Servant

August 27   **Stereotypes**

<u>I free myself from stereotyping.</u>

    I explore my mental images of lesbians and gay men. Are they stereotypes created by heterosexuals? Do I react with approval or disapproval? I have challenged my culture's prescription for love by loving someone of my own gender. I also challenge the rigid definition of beauty by finding others attractive who do not fit the established formula of desirable measurements and features.

    Today I give myself and the world permission to be a myriad assortment. It is all right to be masculine, it is all right to be feminine, and it is all right to be what all of us are in some measure—a blend of masculine and feminine. I allow myself to be unique. Loving myself for being me and you for being you lets us be together without being the same.

    I see beauty in people who appear to fit stereotypes, but their beauty does not result from having a pre-determined collection of features—it comes from their willingly being themselves. I treasure differentness and sameness and all creation. This is a true liberation of the spirit.

August 28   **Sexual Orientation**

    What everyone needs to do is respect the deep-seated knowledge in each of us about our sexuality, and I think there is nothing wrong with heterosexuals at all!

                                                                                      Elizabeth Birch
                                                                           quoted by Pam Walton
                                                                       Out in Suburbia [video]

August 29   **Sexual Orientation**

<u>I affirm my same-sex loving.</u>

    Developing self-love is a lifelong task. In my same-sex orientation, I have an especially difficult obstacle to self-love, living in a culture that tells me I am evil, sick, or perverted. I reject those false judgments in my mind, but they are harder to erase from my heart.

    Truly loving myself means accepting my sexual orientation as a lovable part of myself. I seek out lesbians and gay men showing their love, and I marvel at their beauty. The goodness in those people is evident, and I recognize the same goodness within myself.

    I am fine just the way I am. It is the world that needs to change, so I can be safe and free in my loving. I claim love for myself, my whole self, and challenge the world to let my love transform it.

August 30   **Breaking Up**

When you see me backing off and pulling away
It's 'cause I love you
Guess that I don't know how to be just friends
You see me backing off and pulling away
It's 'cause I love you
I'm an actress, but I don't know how to pretend

Holly Near
"Backing Off and Pulling Away"
Watch Out [audio recording]

August 31   **Breaking Up**

<u>I give myself the space I need in separating.</u>

    I rise to the challenge of respecting what I need at the end of a relationship. Breaking up with a lover in the lesbian and gay community can be especially painful because of the greater probability of encountering each other. I may find myself giving up activities that I enjoy, avoiding places that have been important to me because I fear seeing my ex-lover. Losing the relationship then becomes only a part of the loss.

    I listen to my inner voice that tells me when I need to avoid contact with my ex-lover. It can be healthy to be away from that person as I heal. Perhaps we need to have separate circles permanently. At the same time, I consider the possibility that at some point I may be able to have a friendship with my ex-partner. We have much in common—otherwise we would not have come together as lovers.

    I move beyond any sense of failure and remind myself I did the best I could, given the situation. Even though this love did not last, I am still a worthwhile, lovable person, and I treat myself with gentleness during my healing process.

    There is no right or wrong way to go through a separation, only what is healthy and respectful for me and my ex-partner. I let myself know what works best for me and take the time and space I need for healing.

September

September 1   **Sexual Self-Love**

My finger tips run over my body - gently as I study the curves I know as me - the protrusions and movements of my still watery body. My skin flows the essence of magic into my hands and somehow I know all is well, every inch - every touch - every inch of my sensual naked watery body.

Sue Schlangen
untitled poem
April, 1994

September 2   Sexual Self-Love

I take care of myself sexually.

Recognizing the importance of the sexual component in my self-love, I combat the negative messages I have received regarding masturbation, just as I have fought the stigma of same-sex orientation.

I think about what I have learned through pleasuring myself sexually. No one knows my body as well as I do, and when I am open to touching my physical self, I learn what gives me sexual satisfaction. With privacy and imagination, I explore what gives me pleasure. I let myself know that masturbation as my total sexual experience is a valid choice of which I don't need to be ashamed. I can choose to be self-sufficient.

If I desire a sexual relationship with another person but am not finding it at this point in my life, I consider the advantages of masturbation. It is much more than a substitute for sexual contact with another person. I know how to please myself better than a lover, and I use my alone times for increasing self-intimacy. Masturbation is safe sex, and what I learn in making love to myself enhances possible future sexual relationships with others.

Today I choose myself as my lover. Exploring my sexuality in this way challenges my creativity. I can be "me-sexual" for now!

September 3   Inner Voice

I have come to this: I may not have control, mastery, skill, talent or any of those necessary literary things. But what I do have is a passionate, stubborn desire to find my own voice. I could spend my life struggling to find it; not to write like anyone I admire, or as I was told I should, or on any of the "great" subjects, but simply to speak authentically about my experience. That's why being rich and famous isn't important except as it encourages you to go on with that struggle process, not "expressing" yourself, but creating yourself, in a different form.

Esther Newton, writing as "Pauline"
Womenfriends: A Soap Opera

September 4   Inner Voice

My inner voice tells me my truth.

During some periods of self-examination, it was tempting to ignore the inner voice telling me about my sexual orientation. I told myself I couldn't possibly be homosexual. Trying to override the truth of who I am, I devised rationalizations: it's just a phase; I'm simply admiring a nice body; we're only friends.

Little by little, though, I have learned to hear the real messages in me: my same-sex orientation is my natural state; I am attracted to people of the same gender; we are lovers. Hearing these truthful voices within me, I am learning that it doesn't work to ignore my reality. Accepting who I am, no matter how difficult, is easier than pretending to be someone else. As I accept my same-sex orientation, I am finding an inner congruity that allows me to celebrate the revelations of my heart, to trust their rightness for my life, and to love myself for who I really am.

September 5   **Valuing the Past**

I love my past. I love my present. I'm not ashamed of what I've had, and I'm not sad because I have it no longer.

Colette
The Last of Chéri

September 6   **Valuing the Past**

<u>I am enriched by both the joy and pain of my past.</u>

My past is a mosaic of dark and light. Wouldn't it be better just to forget the difficult times? In my same-sex orientation, it seems that I've had more than my share of hurts, struggles, and unhappiness.

I can't block out all the negatives in my past without losing the good memories too. I savor the happy experiences—moments of closeness, celebration, silliness, peacefulness. They have brought me joy and reason to look forward to the future.

Both my good and bad experiences are part of my history. I remind myself that growth has come out of the struggle. As I have suffered, I have developed sensitivity and become stronger.

When I look at myself in that light, I see my scars as beautiful, and I treasure the hard times. My wisdom did not come easily—I proudly remember the whole of my past.

September 7   **Seeing Options**

Today I courageously unlock all the doors of possibility in my mind. I am free to be and express all that I am.

Perry Tilleraas
The Color of Light

September 8   **Seeing Options**

<u>I am open to the choices before me.</u>

I look at my decision-making power. While I accept the reality that some aspects of my life are beyond my control as a result of my same-sex orientation, I don't need to be a victim. There are many choices open to me: how out to be, how to find support for who I am, how to shape my life in a way that affirms who I am.

Taking responsibility for what I can control sets me on the course I want for my life. All my options can be viewed as opportunities when I approach them with optimism. I choose to think and act positively.

I am ready to see myself as having the ability and decisiveness to shape my future. Today I think creatively about my vision and plan ways of achieving it. I move into my power with confidence and enthusiasm.

September 9 — Supportive Caring

Cleaving is an activity which should be left to snails for cleaning ponds and aquariums. Multiplicity of relationships does not create the number of conflicts the morality tales of our culture would have us believe if the basis of each relationship is the autonomy of the self and the freedom of the other.

Jane Rule
Lesbian Images

September 10 — Supportive Caring

<u>I am respectful in my caring.</u>

The people in my life are important to me. I enjoy helping them, but sometimes I can do *too* much. When that happens, I become a self-appointed savior that keeps those I love from being the best they can be. I am being controlling when I take over what others are capable of doing for themselves. I am disrespectful of myself and others if I lend a hand from a sense of duty instead of a desire to help.

I have experienced much pain, sometimes related to my sexual orientation and sometimes related to other difficulties. It makes sense that I would want to protect others from the pain I have felt, but I must allow others the dignity of making their own decisions and living with the consequences. Experiencing pain and growing through it is a necessary part of everyone's existence. My advice may be helpful, and I can be supportive, but my loved ones must ultimately deal with their challenges themselves.

Staying present with others, I respect them as independent individuals. I care without controlling—that is real love.

September 11 — Complexity of Self

We have to dare to be ourselves, however frightening or strange that self may prove to be.

May Sarton
Mrs. Stevens Hears the Mermaids Singing

September 12 — Complexity of Self

<u>My being is a blend of many energies.</u>

I defy description. My self is full of contradictions, shadings, changes, inconsistencies, subtleties. Labels can be useful, but they don't define me. Many people would like me to be easily categorized. I can't be put into a neat little box—spilling out, I move with the cosmos. My being consists of millions of molecules keeping time to the rhythms of the universe.

My self-exploration yields new discoveries—I accept them without having to catalog. Today I embrace all of who I am—including the parts I don't yet understand. Looking forward to the surprises of my blossoming personhood, I am grateful for complicated me.

September 13 — Strength

It is not necessary to be hard
to be strong

soft is in order
for those of us who have known
boundaries enough to live what is given,
up beyond isolation
burning
of broken-ness & death
& children & women & men weeping

tenderness too, is survival
lived through

Kayla Collins
"Quilt Poem, II"
Search

September 14 — Strength

<u>I celebrate my well-earned strength.</u>

Because of my same-sex orientation, I have had to struggle against waves of condemnation for who I am, and I have survived. Today I celebrate the strength I have gained on this difficult journey. Although I would not choose suffering, I recognize my growth as a result of these experiences. I give myself credit for facing these obstacles and finding ways of overcoming them.

Everyone deals with problems, and I have further trials in my future. However, now that I am stronger, I take each new step with greater resolve. If I lived yesterday with grace, how much better will I deal with today and tomorrow? Knowing that my strength will see me through, I move forward with confidence.

September 15   **Clarifying Relationships**

It certainly can be confusing. Friends become lovers; former lovers become friends; friends become lovers with our lovers; our lovers become lovers with our friends' lovers, and on it goes. The boundaries can become very fuzzy.

JoAnn Loulan
Lesbian Passion

September 16   **Clarifying Relationships**

I am becoming more clear about sexual and non-sexual relationships.

In a world where almost everything is sexualized, I have the option of keeping some of my relationships non-sexual. However, I need to be intentional about what I want in order to have clarity. My same-sex loving opens me to wide possibilities for love and friendship. Since any same-sex relationship has the potential of being sexual, I have the choice of whether to pursue this option with any particular person.

When a friendship takes on sexual overtones, I must decide whether that is what I want. If one person wants a friend and the other wants a lover, can the relationship survive? If I am in a monogamous relationship and feel sexually attracted to a friend, am I open about it to my lover and my friend? So many aspects to consider!

I can acknowledge sexual feelings without acting on them. Sometimes simply the acknowledgment changes my feelings, and only when I recognize my true emotions can I be clear about what I want to do. Whether I admit my sexual feelings to others or not is my choice, but I need to be honest with myself.

I accept the challenge of dealing with the complexities of the sexual and non-sexual—in feelings, intentions, and actions. I value all of my connections with people and approach the range of my relationships with bold integrity.

September 17   **Outing**

I think everyone must leave the closet sometime. I'm not the person to harm those that are not ready by dragging them out, but I think they are hurting us all by not coming forward....Liberace could have done incalculable good!

Leonard Matlovich
quoted by Troy Perry and Thomas Swicegood
Profiles in Gay and Lesbian Courage

September 18 — Outing

I deal with outing issues according to my personal ethics.

I observe situations of "outing," revealing someone's same-sex orientation without that person's permission. I think about times I have been outed. The instances may have proven harmful to me, or they may have cleared the way to closer relationships with those involved. Regardless of the result, there was a sense of betrayal, powerlessness, and loss of privacy.

I consider whether there are situations in which I feel outing is justified. If closeted lesbians or gay men in positions of authority are deliberately exposing or oppressing other lesbians and gay men, do they still have a right to their own privacy? Are there AIDS-related issues in which outing is necessary to protect others? I must find my own answers to these difficult questions as I define my personal ethics and weigh individual rights against the interdependence of humanity.

Today I consider how I respect others' privacy. I also consider the special obligations of all those who exercise power over others. I visualize a society where all people, regardless of their station in life, act with integrity and with concern for the common good. As I seek to honor myself and others, I am moving towards that vision.

September 19 — Fear and Courage

I've made a very conscious decision in my life when I was going through a lot of changes after I got divorced, that...I was not going to do something because I was afraid, and I was not going to do something because other people thought I shouldn't do it. I was only going to do it because of me, and if it was right for me, I was going to do it.

Marilyn Gum
quoted by Pam Walton
Out in Suburbia [video]

September 20 — Fear and Courage

I am courageous even when I am afraid.

Being afraid is a natural and protective response to danger. It prepares my body to deal with threats to my well-being. I need courage to handle such situations, but my fear remains. There is no reason to be ashamed when I am afraid or when I choose to retreat from a situation—flight may be the wisest decision at times.

Living takes special bravery because of society's hostility to my sexual orientation. I risk discrimination, harassment, even death, on a daily basis. Today I let myself experience all my feelings freely. Centering myself, I listen to the guidance of my inner voice. With fear, valor, and wisdom, I move ahead in my life.

September 21   Taking Stock

> *Most living things*
> *need to succumb*
> *to the harshness of winter,*
> *before budding again*
> *in the spring.*

Margareth Cecilia Miller
"Breakdown"
Journeys

September 22   Taking Stock
Autumnal Equinox

I celebrate the autumn harvest of wisdom in my soul.

    The autumnal equinox is a time of balance, when the light and dark hours are equal. It is a time for harvesting the bounty of the summer and preparing for the harsh winter ahead.

    I look at the balance I am achieving in my life—finding joy in the light, growing strong with the dark. My harvest is what I have learned through my laughter and tears. Because of my same-sex loving, I have been given many opportunities for growth. I am not thankful for injustice and persecution, but I can appreciate the ways I have grown in dealing with difficult experiences. I feel gratitude for the special gifts born out of my pain—close relationships, invincible strength, new courage, deep sensitivity, communion with the universe.

    I know that both more harvests and more winters lie ahead in the seasons of my life. The gifts from my past are the resources I bring to my future. As I ready myself for challenging times, I gather an awareness of my riches through this autumnal celebration.

September 23   Taking Stock
Autumnal Equinox

This is how I've grown this past summer:_____

_____

_____

These are the inner resources I have for the approaching winter:_____

_____

_____

_____

September 24 — Community

By liberating the family and basing it on love, we also liberate our community. Duty freely given provides us with a community based on trust and honor, not greed or self-aggrandizement. We again set ourselves apart from a society beset by the very problems we are finding the answers to.

Jean-Nickolaus Tretter
"Redefining Family"
Official Pride Guide, Twin Cities, 1993

September 25 — Community

<u>I bond with lesbians and gay men in a community based on love.</u>

I am linked to other lesbians and gay men through my same-sex loving as well as through the oppression all of us have suffered. These connections draw us together despite our diversity. We find a sense of community with each other, a feeling of intimacy that both comforts and energizes.

How would this bond be changed if there were no homophobia? If our unity exists merely to fight a common foe, our connections with each other will serve no purpose once our enemy is gone. As a people of love, though, we are rising above the negativity. We are building coalitions that unite people through compassion and positive action. We are helping to create a new paradigm of what it means to be *human*, and our communal bonds will continue even when we are no longer oppressed.

I treasure all that we share. I am moving beyond pain into love, and into a better world for all.

September 26 — Love for My Body

I recently saw a blue jean advertisement directed at teenagers that said, "Maybe it's not your body you need to change. Maybe it's your blue jeans." I thought, "Thank heaven!"

JoAnn Loulan
Lesbian Passion

September 27 — Love for My Body

<u>I explore the beauty of my body.</u>

I can love my body, even though it isn't the "ideal" portrayed on television, in movies and in store windows. Rising above negative messages about how I "should" look and move, I develop a multiple definition of beauty. I affirm that my body is beautiful:

large or small, old or young, missing some parts, or moving in a different way, whatever! Wherever I fall along any continuum fits within my new parameters of attractiveness.

I stand naked before a mirror and look for just one feature I can love. Each time I look deeply at myself, I find another part to admire. I challenge myself to see beauty, even in those aspects I believe are ugly.

Today I let myself love my whole body. As my sexual orientation is different from many, but fine, so my body is different from many, but distinctly lovable.

September 28 — Minority Status

We are not out of the mainstream, we are part of the mainstream. We are not obvious, but we "pass" every day as heterosexual. While some may see it as an asset, our ability to "pass" and to hide has perhaps been our greatest liability. More than anything else, the closet has kept us from being accepted and respected for who we actually are.

Rob Eichberg
Coming Out—An Act of Love

September 29 — Minority Status

I celebrate my minority status.

As I think of what it means to be same-sex oriented, I can focus on what it means to give up the benefits of being straight, or I can accept the gifts of being who I truly am. I am released from the heterosexual myths and pressure to conform. Because no one pushes me to marry my same-sex partner, I decide whether or not I want a committed relationship, and what level of commitment is right for me. Becoming a parent is more of a challenge, but it is never an accident. I have a special bond with others of same-sex orientation because of our commonality.

It's natural to desire being part of the mainstream. Today, though, I appreciate the rewards of being in the out-group, and I acknowledge that whatever the advantages or disadvantages, I need to be me.

September 30 — Created Family

I believe that I live in a family, too. My partner and I constitute a family. Many gay and lesbian people have created families just as heterosexual people have. We're not against families. We think families are wonderful. Many of us live in either families that we've created or families that we were born into, and we cherish those relationships.

Alan Spear, Minnesota state senator
Star Tribune, Minneapolis-St. Paul

October

October 1   **Created Family**

<u>I create a new concept of a love partnership.</u>

    Who are my family members? Creating family through marriage is an age-old process, but just because I can't marry legally doesn't mean I'm not a family with my lover. My creative process goes far beyond the confines of traditional marriage, though, as I develop an innovative concept of a love partnership.

    If I desire the closeness of a long-term commitment, I have the opportunity of doing so without the baggage of stereotypes—dominance of one partner over the other, inequality of shared responsibilities, economic power-wielding, unrealistic visions of eternal ecstasy, unhealthy codependency. I can work for equality, respect, real-world expectations, and healing interactions.

    Relationships are adventures, and I accept the challenge to define my partnership in creative and healthy ways. I add hope and determination and an open mind to my caring, and there it is—an evolutionary family!

October 2   **Changing Self**

*   When we change how we live and what we do with our energy, we modify our own structure. If we act no differently today from the way we acted yesterday, there is no basis for change. But through our efforts at working on recovery, if we perform in new ways and think new thoughts, we become ourselves catalysts of change.*

                                                                              Sheppard Kominars
                                                                              Accepting Ourselves

October 3   **Changing Self**

<u>As I change myself, I transform the world.</u>

    I would like to wave a magic wand and create a world of harmony, equality, justice, and love! I long for all of it to happen.

    Although I can't mold the world as I wish, I can change myself, and as I alter myself, my environment changes in response to the differences in me. I cannot choose, or even predict how those around me will change, but there will be positive aspects. As I go about my life process, I am having a constructive effect on all that touches me.

    Looking at what I want for myself, I vow not to change simply for the sake of change. If others try to change me, I am firm in rejecting whatever doesn't fit my plan. Only I can decide who I am becoming, and I move toward my goals. When my growth is right for me, ripples of healing radiate outward from me.

Today I have faith in forward motion. I am becoming my best self, and that self is helping to birth a better universe.

October 4 — Sexuality

Healthy sex is any sexual activity between two consenting adults that is not harmful to them or to others.... God has done a great thing: We come fully equipped, no batteries needed, to share our joy and our human be-ing—mentally, emotionally, and physically. The only restriction we have been given is inherent in the equipment: keep it healthy, don't abuse it, "play nice," and respect each other's toys.

Tina Tessina
Gay Relationships for Men and Women

October 5 — Sexuality

How I communicate with my body is a beautiful part of me.

Rejecting the cultural pronouncements that condemn me in my same-sex loving, I assert that what I do with my body is wonderful. I respect myself and others when I express myself sexually in the way that is intrinsic to my being. I am in charge of my body, and I decide what actions are right for me.

With pride and without shame, I participate in the adventure of bodies moving together, sharing intimacy, giving and receiving pleasure. In a world that glorifies the ugliness of hate and violence, I celebrate the loveliness I work through my physical self. My sexual lovemaking affirms all that is splendid in me and others who are true to their natural sexuality.

October 6 — AIDS Quilt

You know, I sometimes look at his picture on my desk, and I think, "Where the hell are you?" He's got to be somewhere, right? And it's been almost three years now since Jeffrey died, and still every day I wonder where he is. For me, the Quilt is where Jeff is.

Vito Russo
quoted by Rob Epstein and Jeffrey Friedman
Common Threads [film]

October 7 — AIDS Quilt

I experience healing and love through the Quilt.

Seeing The Names Project Quilt brings up many strong emotions: overwhelming sadness at the thousands of lives that have been lost; shared love with all who cared for these memorialized lives; mourning for the loss of what might have been; awe for all the tenderness woven into these panels; joy that these people have not been forgotten but live on in the panels and in the hearts of those who journeyed with them. Bringing these emotions into consciousness heals me and lets me move ahead in my life.

Today I let the power of love strengthen my faith that all of our lives constitute a huge power and a real energy that can bring about goodness and beauty for the present, and in whatever may lie beyond.

I let myself grieve through the Quilt. I let myself love through the Quilt. I celebrate life through the Quilt.

October 8 — Passion

Passion is a source of greatness within each of us. This is true of great works of art, great deeds of service and the ordinary greatness required to love ourselves and other people on a daily basis. We begin to glimpse the power of our passion when we march in a Take Back The Night rally; express our own form of spirituality; or assert our rights to inseminate, give birth and raise children as we choose. "What has passion to do with choosing an art form?" Gertrude Stein once asked. "Everything!"

JoAnn Loulan
Lesbian Passion

October 9 — Passion

<u>I claim my passionate nature.</u>

Passion often refers to sexual fervor, but my passion extends into all areas of my being. My life is in balance when I recognize that I feel creative passion for my beliefs, my work, my recreation, and my friends, as well as for my lovers. My multiple passions empower me in my wholeness.

At times when I feel most alive, my sexual feelings are a part of my zest. They are integrated into my passion for living as a part of my self-expression. I revel in my sexual passion as a healthy aspect of who I am, giving special affirmation to my natural same-sex desires.

Today I acknowledge my strong emotions, even fiery depths, and appreciate the energy and creativity they bring to the exciting person I am. Feeling pride in my vitality, I celebrate the spirited intensity of my passionate self.

October 10 — Coming Out

While every day is an opportunity to tell the truth, October 11 is a day for paying special attention to our progress in coming out—and for making a difference in the way homosexuality is viewed and experienced by all of us.

Rob Eichberg
Coming Out—An Act of Love

October 11   **Coming Out**
National Coming Out Day

<u>I find courage for my coming-out process in community with others.</u>

As I see others around me finding the courage to come out today, I consider my readiness for further self-revelation. I don't pressure myself into something I'm not prepared for, but the designation of a day for coming out may give me the incentive I need to expand the group of those who know my sexual orientation.

One person proclaims to the people on the bus to work that he is gay. At a press conference, an actress announces she is a lesbian. An aging mother listens as her son finds the strength to come out to her. Confiding to her best friend, a courageous teenager reveals her same-sex attractions.

I choose my time and find my own way of coming out. With whom do I long to share my truth? Perhaps my coming-out process for today is giving messages to myself, a dialogue with myself about my loving. Whatever my way of celebrating this holiday, I recognize its significance in furthering lesbian and gay pride—within myself, within the circle of my contacts, within a world that is being challenged to face the facts of my presence and my beautiful loving.

October 12   **Celebrating Truth**
Columbus Day

...Whatever speaks the truth of our hearts can only make us stronger. We must be the last generation to live in silence.

Paul Monette
The New York Times

<u>I work to create holidays based on truth.</u>

As people celebrate this day as Columbus Day, I am reminded of how history has been distorted. Columbus' cruel treatment of native Americans has been ignored, just as hate crimes against lesbians and gay men have been denied. The U.S. Government's persecution of native Americans has been translated into political expediencies, just as vengeance against lesbians and gay men has been veiled in religious jargon.

I won't pretend such torture did not occur or that it was justified. Instead I celebrate truth on this day, commemorating the strength and bravery of those who have suffered innocently throughout the ages. As I work for an honest rewriting of history, I dedicate my efforts to bringing about justice and equality in the world.

Having seen my own reality ignored and discounted, I bring my personal experiences to the struggle of all oppressed people. With courage and pride, I reject holidays of lies, and create holidays of integrity.

October 13 — Taking Risks

This expedition has been a dramatic example of what happens each day of my life in my pursuits. I simply must trust my heart and follow my path as I strive for my goals and destinations. Each step has a certain amount of uncertainty and risk.

Ann E. Bancroft
unpublished journal entry
Women's Trans-Antarctic Expedition, 1992-1993

October 14 — Taking Risks

<u>I dare to share myself with others.</u>

I need other people, and they need me. Having suffered rejection because of my same-sex orientation or for other reasons, I am tempted to isolate myself. Permanently withdrawing, though, isn't the answer.

Today I reach within me for the daring to be open with others. Studying the people in my life, I choose carefully the ones I approach. I test the waters rather than diving in. Little by little, I risk the intimacy I desire.

When I fear rejection, I remind myself of my worth. Knowing me enriches the lives of those I touch. I deserve to be listened to, to be taken seriously, to be valued for who I am.

There are people who are safe to be with. I choose those who appreciate the beautiful person I am and who help me to like myself. As I share who I am with others, I learn about myself. I am letting myself be an important member of the human family.

October 15 — Surviving Abuse

Congratulate yourself for breaking the cycle of abuse.

Ricki Geiger
Empowerment for Lesbians

October 16 — Surviving Abuse

<u>I am strong enough to move beyond abuse.</u>

I am ready to heal from the abuse I have experienced, whether it was sexual, physical, emotional, or spiritual. In my enduring strength, I am determined to face what has happened to me and move past it into the productive life I envision for myself.

The task is especially difficult if my abuser was someone of the same sex. I want to believe that lesbians and gay men don't victimize each other. Today I accept that I can go on with my life without denying who I am. I remind myself that I don't have to be like my abuser. I will need help in my healing process, but I can be healthy and non-abusive in my same-sex loving.

The sexual identity of my abuser is ultimately irrelevant—how I deal with the abuse is what matters. When I am being mistreated, I find ways of protecting myself. If a relationship continues to feel abusive, I need to leave. I seek professional counseling. I am taking the necessary steps because I know I deserve to be treated with respect. As I recognize and act on my truths, I am getting healthier. The will to survive and to feel good is taking me to where I want to go.

October 17   **Breaking Up**

> *I know now*
> *there will be other loves.*
> *These scars simply mark*
> *this passage of my journey.*
> *I shall raise my head*
> *toward the mountains.*
> *The moisture on my face*
> *will simply be the cleansing rain.*
>
> Margareth Cecilia Miller
> from poem "Moving On"
> *Journeys*

October 18   **Breaking Up**

<u>I show love for myself and respect for my ex-lover in ending a relationship.</u>

I stay centered through the time of breaking up with my lover. It would be easy to let the pain of ending my relationship degenerate into destructive anger, unnecessary blaming, seeking revenge, or harboring bitter resentment. But I can rise above such negativity. Not having the option of divorce as a legal channel for settling impasses, I accept the challenge to be creative in resolving differences as I separate from my lover.

Today I remember that I can respect myself and my ex-partner, even when I am not being treated respectfully, even when I am angry. If outside support is needed, I seek guidance through mediators, therapists, trustworthy friends and helpful family members. Calling upon my inner strength, I find fresh wisdom for the moment. As I move through the struggle, I am loving myself. I remember to honor myself in my aloneness and when I interact with my ex-partner.

I am finding new ways of living in this world, especially in the difficult times. While I am learning that love between two people may not endure, my self-love continues and grows and brings the promise of better tomorrows back to my heart.

October 19 — Being Single

It's hard for some people to imagine someone can be happy single. We need to open up our acceptance for other kinds of happiness.

Chuck Collins
quoted by Deb Price
The Detroit News

October 20 — Being Single

<u>I am an independent person who can choose to be single.</u>

In a culture that idealizes the heterosexual couple, I am doubly defiant if I claim my same-sex orientation and also choose to be single. My sexual orientation is labeled by the gender I am attracted to, but I don't have to be in a relationship—now or ever. I can lead a full and satisfying life alone if I choose. Perhaps I have a mission in life that has no room for a partner. If I am a private person, the serenity in my aloneness may be vital to my well-being. It may be this is a time in my life that requires all my energy for myself and my own growth.

If I have thoughts about wanting to be part of a couple, I let myself know that option is open to me. I remind myself that I deserve and am capable of healthy, caring relationships. People are necessary in my life—acquaintances, friends, biological or created family—but not necessarily a lover or committed partner.

I am a strong and independent person. As with all people, I experience times of loneliness —in or out of a relationship—but I also know the value of solitude. If I decide I want an intimate sexual relationship, I bring a beautiful, healthy self to my loving. But for today, I revel in my own completeness. My self-love is the love that makes me whole.

October 21 — Patience with Others

I want to share my life with you and trust you will accept it, even if you don't understand right away....I suggest that you first become confident and comfortable about my homosexuality before you discuss it with others. Then what they think is what they think and your reaction can come from understanding rather than from the fear of defending, justifying, or seeing it as a problem.

"Jennifer"
Christine Heron Stockton
Lesbian Letters

October 22 — Patience with Others

I give others time to develop understanding and acceptance.

As I am learning to be gentle with myself, I must also learn to be gentle with others. Having come to terms with my sexual orientation within myself, I want the whole world to accept it too. I may be impatient with friends and family, employers and coworkers, government agencies and laws that don't accept me for who I am. I have a right to that acceptance, but I also know that my internal coming-out process took time, and I must give others that time to alter their attitudes as well as their actions.

As I deal with others, I define my bottom line—what I can tolerate and what is unacceptable. I refuse to be treated disrespectfully by friends and family. If those in my life are staunchly against me, I may need to separate myself from them. However, if they are struggling with homophobia, perhaps I can help them in their process by staying present and offering my wisdom.

When government officials waver, I continue to write letters, protest and march. Times are changing, and I am contributing to the progress of human rights.

Respect for my own limits is important, but today I also have patience as I respect the process that others must also go through.

October 23 — Power from Within

Let me listen to me and not to them.

Gertrude Stein
quoted by JoAnn Loulan
Lesbian Passion

October 24 — Power from Within

In exploring myself, I discover my spiritual power.

My spirituality is core to my being; at times I may deny it or lose touch with it, but my life is enriched when I center myself and commune with my own vital force.

I am ready to give myself quiet time to explore the depths of my being and learn who I am. As I develop intimacy with myself, I don't have to be afraid of what I will find. There is goodness and light and beauty deep within. The darkness dwells there, too, but I am strong enough to embrace it all. As I face every aspect of myself, I give myself love and acceptance, and I free myself to grow.

In my same-sex loving, society has encouraged me to deny who I am. Today I separate myself from the destructive messages the world tries to impose on me, and create my own standard. There are parts of me I dislike, but my sexual orientation is not one of them. As I sort out what is hard to accept, I gently acknowledge my imperfections. I am lovable in my humanity. Facing my faults, I accept them as part of who I am. I let my inner force guide me toward what is intended in my life. I am getting in touch with my spirituality. My path is unique—the sacredness within shows me the way.

Lavender Reflections

October 25   **Lovemaking**

When I am making love with myself or a partner, this feels natural:_____

_____

_____

This is what I would like to try:_____

_____

_____

October 26   **Lovemaking**

<u>I am creative in my lovemaking.</u>

    What *do* I do in bed?—the question all heterosexuals supposedly want to ask! I don't need to answer them, but it is important to feel comfortable about my lovemaking. There is no right way or wrong way to make love with myself or with my same-sex partner. I don't need a sex manual to tell me how to express my sexuality.

    I claim my right to ignore everything except what I decide is safe and right for me. I am respectful of my partner and want our pleasure to be mutual. I am free of the cultural expectation of intercourse in the missionary position, and I may cast off other arbitrary restrictions as well.

    Out with the sex manuals! Out with the statistics of who does what! Out with my inner messages of how it "should" to be done!

    In with my fantasies! In with experimenting! In with finding whatever pleases me and my lover, real or imagined!

    With a sense of excitement, I enter a new world of adventure. Who would have guessed how tantalizing sexual creativity can be?

October 27   **Fear of Anger**

    Our fear of anger is a barometer of how badly we want to be, but are scared of being, in mutual relation.

Carter Heyward
Touching Our Strength

October 28 — Fear of Anger

<u>I face my fear of anger.</u>

In a world that discriminates against me in my same-sex orientation, I have many reasons to feel angry. However, such a powerful emotion can be frightening. Sometimes I pretend I don't feel anything; at other times, my rage is so strong I am afraid it will destroy me or those I love. How can I deal with my fear of this powerful force within me?

Today I recognize all my emotions as natural signs of life. Acknowledging my anger is the first step to harnessing its energy, and when I am in control of myself, my fear lessens. As I become healthier, I am dealing with my anger in ways that build, not tear down. I am conquering my fear by finding safe places to express strong emotions and people who are secure enough to accept me when I am angry as long as I am not abusive.

Fear is also a powerful emotion. I am learning from all my emotions, especially those that move fiercely within me.

October 29 — Affirming Relationships

Lack of social and family sanction has left us with few resources to draw upon in maintaining even the most committed of relationships....A relationship which rests upon the support of friends, community and family is one which can more easily survive the difficulties inevitable in long-term partnerships.

Becky Butler
Ceremonies of the Heart

October 30 — Affirming Relationships

<u>I celebrate long-term relationships.</u>

In a culture where many relationships are short-lived, I want to support, and be supported, in ones that endure. I may be tempted to avoid coupled friends when I am single, or forget single friends when I am in a relationship, but I remind myself that the proverbial "three's a crowd" concept isn't always valid.

I need all my friends regardless of the sexual relationships any of us chooses. My life is enriched by the people I know, and I bring my gifts to them as well. On some level we are all role models for each other, as each of us changes and grows.

In a world of limited support for same-sex relationships, I develop durable systems to nurture loving relationships, whether mine or others'. I am bringing stability to an unstable world, not by expecting relationships to last forever, but by celebrating those that touch me and embracing their value.

I find hope in friends who continue loving each other among the struggles of life, and I participate with them as part of an enduring community.

Eleanor Ruth Wagner 113

October 31   Spirituality
Halloween

Fear of being branded a witch eventually silenced the Puritans' assertive women. Fear of being similarly misunderstood has long kept gay people quiet. But now we've begun to speak the truth of gay reality as if our lives depended on it. Perhaps they do.
Deb Price
The Detroit News

I am in touch with my spiritual powers.

Halloween—a blend of many traditions: Celtic Festival of Samhain, lord of death; Autumn Festival of Pomona, Roman goddess of fruit and trees; Christian All-Hallows Eve. On this holiday I honor death as part of the spiral of life. I remember the spiritual people who were accused of witchcraft and persecuted by those who feared them.

Because of my same-sex orientation, I am in solidarity with those oppressed as witches. I grieve that their spirituality was seen as evil, for I am a spiritual person and can use my sacred power for goodness and healing as they did.

Today I celebrate all that I am, while letting myself feel the pain so many of us have suffered. I grieve the loss of lives, and yet feel joy in the cycle of life that promises a new energy rising from the earth. As many people mark this holiday, I sense my power, both alone and in concert with those who dance by my side throughout the world. Our music cannot be silenced. My spirituality transcends the might of my oppressors.

November

November 1   Working with Others

Being human, we have not been able to avoid conflict and hurting one another. We have had to learn two essential characteristics of love: forgiveness and a humble spirit. We had to learn to forgive one another and come to know our own need for forgiveness.
John J. McNeil
Taking a Chance on God

November 2   Working with Others

I support strong lesbian and gay organizations.

I need organizations that work for my interests, and I can be part of the process of making them viable. With the reputation that lesbian and gay groups have for self-destructing, maintaining strong organizations takes special effort by all of us. What can I do to help?

I can look at how I mistrust those in leadership positions. Again and again, leaders have let me down. I have good reason to be mistrustful, but I know there are some people in power who are sensitive to my concerns. As I discover leaders who are trustworthy, I let go of some of my need to control, and give them the support they need to work effectively. I am becoming a constructive participant.

I also look at the extent to which I can be a leader. I have the potential to acquire leadership skills, whether on a large or small scale. I am learning to be active in group processes and to accept responsibility in the organizations that are important to me.

Today I affirm that I have a right to groups who work for my interests. I don't have to be part of oppressing myself or others simply because oppression is what I have known. Supporting organizations that affirm same-sex orientation supports myself too. I give others the right to be human and make mistakes, while accepting them as contributing members of my community. I am a growing, constructive member of a community that is becoming stronger each day.

November 3 — Being a Teenager

The easiest thing to do is get discouraged, and it won't help any if I tell you not to. Try to recapture how happy your gay feelings make you, and how you enjoy being with other gay friends who are like you and know how you feel, or remember how it feels to be with your lover. If you haven't had a lover, well then, you have something to look forward to.

Liza
quoted by Ann Heron
One Teenager in Ten

November 4 — Being a Teenager

<u>I grow stronger and wiser through the trials of my teen years.</u>

What a great challenge to be a teenager with same-sex attractions! Straight teens have enough struggles, but the isolation in same-sex orientation can be especially hard.

Even when I didn't put a label on myself, I sensed I was different. As I move through times of self-revelation, feelings of confusion and insecurity are natural. Now that I am coming to an acceptance of who I am, different emotions are developing— relief, peace, pride, confidence.

When my resources seem limited, I search for new avenues to information and support. When I am pressured by peers or fear rejection, I remind myself of the special human being I am. With ingenuity and perseverance, I look for places where I can feel safe and people who accept or share my sexual orientation.

Despite the pain I experience as a teenager, I am determined to survive, even thrive. I boldly reach out for the tools and supportive people to help me through. I am succeeding. My lifelong process of growing up is underway.

November 5 — Quest for Guidance

To pursue this quest for self, a quest for self-respect, a quest for spiritual fulfillment, we have had to move to a new land, a promised land in our own minds.

Troy Perry
The Lord is my Shepherd and He Knows I'm Gay

November 6 — Quest for Guidance

I march to drummers of love, pride, and truth.

Henry David Thoreau said, "If I seem out of step, I may be listening to a different drummer." In my same-sex orientation, there is no doubt that my journey is very different from many in my culture. Who is the drummer that sets my pace?

Some claim knowledge of a higher power that does not approve of who I am, but I know the truth. Love is the enduring goodness of life, and the love I express in who I am is in synchrony with the universe. I follow the way of love.

Those who work for lesbian and gay rights are also my drummers. There are people in my life who speak words that resonate with my reality—friends, political activists, role models within my community. I am proud to walk with them.

Today I propose the daring idea that *I* am the drummer. Listening to the impulses within my soul, I move in time with my heart. Within me calls a truth I share with those who struggle, who search, who are ready to march.

However I view the journey, I am moving forward among people who hunger for the sound of a strong and true cadence to bring them together. My steps are part of a greater rhythm of enduring love, pride in being, and shared truth.

November 7 — Dealing with Depression

Pain is important: how we evade it, how we succumb to it, how we deal with it, how we transcend it.

Audre Lorde
quoted by Amber Coverdale Sumrall
Write to the Heart

November 8 — Dealing with Depression

I am growing and learning through feelings of depression.

Today I acknowledge that I have good reason to feel depressed some of the time. Whether my issues relate to my sexual orientation or other matters, my reactions are natural and not a sign of weakness. As I name my sadness and sense of hopelessness, I am taking an important step in moving beyond those feelings.

Asking for help is a way of being strong. I can debate whether I could get through this period without outside support, but life is tough enough—why not take advantage of that which facilitates my feeling better?

For now I see my depression as an important part of my growth process. I am learning about myself, life, and what I am here in the world to do. Living with depression is helping me move forward, even when it feels like I'm standing still. I take this time to evaluate what is important to me—what I need in order to be happy and fulfilled.

The decisions aren't easy, but continuing in depression isn't easy either. There is very little I absolutely *must* do. I cast off the "shoulds" inside my head and decide what I *want* to do. Little by little I am taking control of my life. For today I can let myself be, but I know positive changes are coming. They are starting to happen right now.

November 9 — Gender Roles

Quentin Crisp, who has experimented with gender all his life, reveling in his femininity long before it became safe to do so, has said, "Style is just being yourself—on purpose."

Crisp's example challenges us all to explore more possibilities as to who "yourself" might be. For me, it's simply the choice to wear pearls, even with a beard.

William Randall Beard
Equal Time

November 10 — Gender Roles

<u>I define my gender for myself.</u>

My gender was declared at birth by examining my genitals, but gender identity encompasses much more than physical characteristics. In loving someone of my own sex, I have defied an important part of society's definition for my gender role. What other aspects of my gender role differ from my culture's expectations?

Concepts of maleness and femaleness are stereotypes, and no one fits them precisely. I can still feel good about my gender without molding myself into someone I'm not. My feeling about what gender I am comes from deep inside me. With courage I create my own definition and decide the details of playing out my gender identity—how I dress, what I look like, how I move, how I behave. I refuse to be shamed for my same-sex loving or for the way I define my gender. Without making any changes at all, I am a beautiful person—whoever I am, whatever my gender definition, however I choose to live in this world.

November 11
Veterans Day

Peacemaking

> *Don't think you can win anyone with sympathy;*
> *Don't think you can solve things with apology.*
> *Times are hard and people too,*
> *Don't know how it got this way, but more than ever*
> *It's up to me and you....*
> *What will we do if the dream finally ends,*
> *If we lose the chance to make amends?*
> *Gotta take a look at the whole situation...*
> *More than ever we got to.*
>
> Tret Fure
> "It's Up to Me and You"
> *Terminal Hold* [audio recording]

<u>I am a peacemaker today.</u>

On this holiday to remember those who have served in the military, I consider ways of achieving peace in the world. As an oppressed person, I know war can be used as an instrument of oppression in the guise of a quest for justice. As a person who understands about death, I abhor killing.

Today I let myself hope for a world that settles differences without killing. I find ways of resolving conflict with people in my life. In all my life experiences, I strive for compassion, understanding, and open communication. If I can find ways of settling conflict on a person-to-person basis, then there is hope for country-to-country resolutions. By supporting justice, I am working for peace. I am only one person, but my voice joins with those who share a vision, work together, march together, pray together. This voice is heard wherever people listen. I am bringing peace to a weary world today.

November 12

Inconsistency

> *My father asked if I am gay*
> *I asked Does it matter?*
> *He said No not really*
> *I said Yes*
> *He said Get out of my life*
> *I guess it mattered.*
>
> *My boss asked if I am gay*
> *I asked Does it matter?*
> *He said No not really*
> *I told him Yes*
> *He said You're fired, faggot*
> *I guess it mattered.*

> My lover asked Do you love me?
> I asked Does it matter?
> He said Yes
> I told him I love you
> He said Let me hold you in my arms
> For the first time in my life something matters.
>
> My God asked me Do you love yourself?
> I said Does it matter?
> He said Yes
> I said How can I love myself I am gay?
> He said That is the way I made you
> Nothing again will ever matter.
>
> Anonymous

November 13 — Inconsistency

Naming contradictions brings clarity and serenity to my living.

When someone says, "I don't have anything against gays, but...," I know they probably do. Everyone is inconsistent some of the time, but I need people in my life who are consistent on the issues and values that are important to me. I can't afford to be around people who say they accept me but don't, who say they care about me but don't. It is too confusing and damaging to my self-esteem.

I am learning to trust myself when I sense other people's homophobia. I can call them on it or simply make a mental note, but I remind myself that I am seeing through the contradictions. As I recognize its elements in other people, the homophobia within myself is easier to fight.

I maintain my serenity and choose how to use my energy. My options include calling forth my strength to remain in relationship with inconsistent people or walking away from them. I value congruence and people who foster that quality in themselves and others. Each day I achieve more clarity as I strive for consistency in my own life and find it in others.

November 14 — Being Open to Change

> Sometimes it takes a rainy day
> Just to let you know everything's gonna be all right.
> I've been dreaming in the sun, won't you wake me up, someone
> I need a little peace of mind.
> Wake me from this dream that I have dreamed so many times

I need a little peace of mind, oh I need a little peace of mind.
When you open up your life to the living, all things come spilling in on you.
And you're flowing like a river, the Changer and the Changed.
You got to spill some over, spill some over, spill some over, over all.

Cris Williamson
"Waterfall"
The Changer and the Changed [audio recording]

November 15 — Being Open to Change

I embrace change as part of the adventure of living.

So often I must leave parts of my life behind—a job, a friend, a lover, a home, a belief, an era. Even when I choose the change, I have a feeling of loss. Grieving is a natural process, and I let those feelings move through me. Any change is stressful, including those that bring me joy, such as falling in love, buying a house, or starting a new job. I remember to be gentle with myself as I take on more challenges, as well as opportunities for happiness.

Moving beyond the tension, I breathe in the freshness of these beginnings. Life cannot continue without change. I am ready to be truly alive.

I rejoice in the newness of my being. I look at the beautiful person I am today, the one that evolved from yesterday and looks forward to tomorrow.

November 16 — Unconditional Love

I expect my family
to accept me, my
lifestyle, my friends
and my lover.

When they do, they
are not doing anything
extraordinarily open-
minded or brave. They
are, rather, simply
treating me with the
love and respect
I deserve.

Mel White
The Dyke Daily Companion

November 17 — Unconditional Love

I invite people into my life who love me as I am.

As I move through life, I am confronted by reactions to my same-sex loving ranging from abhorrence to admiration. While I can't transform the world, I can choose with whom I interact on a day-to-day basis.

Today I dare to expect more than tolerance from the people around me. I deserve to be loved exactly as I am, to be liked, to have people on my side, whether they are straight, lesbian, gay or bisexual. If friends or family are not supportive, I move on to new systems of nurturing. I know such people exist, and I invite them into my life.

By creating new paradigms in my mind, I am finding new realities in my life. The changes start with me and move steadily outward. I encircle myself with advocates.

November 18 — Beauty of Humanity

When you find someone either attractive or unattractive, examine this feeling to see if it can be traced to the dominant culture's prejudice. See if you can be willing to find many different kinds of bodies attractive.

JoAnn Loulan
Lesbian Passion

November 19 — Beauty of Humanity

I acknowledge that there is beauty in every person.

Do I tend to define beauty only in terms of people similar to myself? Those with low self-esteem may admire only those who are different from themselves. As I grow in wisdom, I am finding loveliness in people I previously considered unattractive. I don't have to like individuals in order to appreciate their beauty, and I know that admiring someone is different from being sexually attracted. With some people, I may need to keep some distance for my self-protection, but I can still recognize their positive points.

As I find something of value in each person, either physical appearance or inner attributes, I am developing a concept of the interconnectedness of all human beings. I am simultaneously uncovering elegance within myself and in those around me. When I get in touch with the bond I share with all living things in the universe, I cannot see any of us as completely devoid of good qualities.

If I have difficulty seeing beauty in another person, I look within myself for my insecurity, my short-sightedness, my self-centeredness. I can rise above my prejudices to appreciate what is positive in those around me. Am I discovering or creating this new view of the world? Both!

November 20   **Participating in Change**

Some of the things I am doing in my own life to make the world better are: _____

_____

_____

_____

_____

November 21   **Participating in Change**

<u>My positive actions improve my own life and the lives of others.</u>

Today I celebrate the forward motion that is occurring in the world and affirm that I am part of the transformation. I can feel frustrated at the slowness of attaining civil rights for lesbians and gay men, yet recognize that some advances are occurring.

Although I have been a victim, I am capable of casting off the victim mentality. I am framing a new place for myself in the universe—one of empowerment and constructive action. I make decisions that change my personal life for the better, and I participate in group processes that encourage change for many people.

More and more, society at large is acknowledging my right to same-sex loving. Throughout the country and world, laws are being passed granting legal protection for my human rights. More people are publicly out than ever before. Issues of sexual orientation are frequently addressed in the media. Straight people in greater numbers are acting as advocates for lesbians and gay men.

My coming-out process is a small part of what is happening, but as many more add their contributions, more significant changes come about. I can be proud of the part I have played as I look forward to the progress of the future.

November 22   **Appreciation**

I have been perfectly happy the way I am. If my mother was responsible for it, I am grateful.

Christopher Isherwood
quoted by Leigh W. Rutledge
Unnatural Quotations

November 23 — Appreciation
Thanksgiving

<u>I am grateful today.</u>

I can appreciate my life without discounting the hard parts. I confront difficulties in my same-sex loving, in my dealing with injustice, in getting through each day. There are blessings as well as hardships in all that I do, in all that happens to me, and in all that the world is.

With gratitude I name the goodness that is mine. I see the positive and negative in the same circumstance. Which do I choose to emphasize? I can pity myself for the hard lot I have been given, or I can see an opportunity and work with it. I can spend my time mourning what never can be, or I can move ahead and make the best of what I have.

Today I dwell on happiness. I take energy from all that benefits me and move forward in the promise of exciting adventures to come. I appreciate my life and what I am called to do with it, starting with the trivial and moving to the momentous. All of it is significant and enhances my existence. Thank you, Universe!

November 24 — Holiday Celebrations

When holidays came—the Fourth of July, Thanksgiving, birthdays, anniversaries, Christmas, and Easter—I had to choose with whom I would spend the time, my family or my lover. It was always tormenting, and always my family came up on the short end of the stick. I was not going to leave my lover alone and cause him unhappiness so that Dad would not be reminded of who I am.

Gilberto Gerald
quoted by Troy Perry and Thomas Swicegood
Profiles in Gay and Lesbian Courage

November 25 — Holiday Celebrations

<u>I design my holiday celebration.</u>

Blessed are those whose families embrace their sexual orientation, for their holidays are true opportunities for celebration. Holidays can be difficult for anyone, but when issues of sexual orientation are involved, they can be especially difficult.

If I am not out, I must deal with the secrecy. I struggle with whether to bring my lover into family celebrations and what label to use—"friend," "roommate," perhaps no label at all.

If I am out, there may still be discomfort—deciding how openly affectionate to be, choosing whether certain topics of conversation are to be avoided, knowing how to deal with silence or homophobic remarks:

"I just wish you didn't have to flaunt it!"
"What did I do to make you this way?"

"Don't tell Grandma—she couldn't handle it!"
If my family does not support me, I may choose to be with them despite the stress, or I may decide I need to spend holidays in other ways. If my family invites me but excludes my partner, I have a difficult choice to make. Whatever I decide, it is right for me. Once my mind is made up, I give myself permission to proceed joyfully. I am in charge of how I spend my holidays. Finding what is meaningful for me, I truly celebrate.

November 26   **Times of Inactivity**

> *Breathing in touches*
> *that drift on the snow,*
> *the memory of colour*
> *and soft perfume*
> *lie heavy with our needing.*
>
> *The sun and pollens*
> *will fly again,*
> *after this time of sleep.*

Margareth Cecilia Miller
"Winter"
Journeys

November 27   **Times of Inactivity**

<u>I give myself time to pause in my life when I need it.</u>
"Move!"—"Faster!"—"Produce!" The messages of a hectic world bombard me. When the pressure becomes too great, I stop and reflect and just hold still. I don't always have to be accomplishing something. There are resting places along the way up each mountain. The pauses prepare me for future forward motion.

If my lack of activity seems prolonged, if I am eager to get on with my life but somehow can't get into forward gear, perhaps I need to ask what is keeping me here. Is the path I've chosen too steep? Are there obstacles I have hesitated to face? Do I need to consider a different path?

The answers may help me be content with staying where I am or energize me to make a change. I remember, though, that motion can be forward, backward, or sideways, and one direction is not necessarily superior to another. Retreat can be a survival tactic when needed. Is my goal to get somewhere or to be satisfied with where I am?

Decisions related to my same-sex orientation may require that I take extra time to nurture myself. I must resist the messages from the world that don't fit me. I won't be pushed, and I won't push myself faster than is right for me.

The speed limit I set is my own. I take my time, but I'm getting to where I need to go all the same.

November 28   **Children in My Life**

Some of the people who hate us think we're out to indoctrinate their children. Frankly, we're trying to save their children from suicide. A third of all teen suicides are gay and lesbian and they're all unnecessary, and we want those kids to have a chance.

Paul Monette
The New York Times

November 29   **Children in My Life**

The beauty of my love is healthy for children to see.

Children see the beauty and warmth of people loving each other, regardless of gender, if they have not been exposed to homophobia. If I accept my same-sex loving as natural and beautiful, I don't have to question when to come out to children. Do heterosexuals ask when they should let their children know they are heterosexual? When do heterosexual parents let their children know they love each other? Hopefully from the moment a child is born! They decide at what point to discuss sexuality, but they teach love by living it with their families.

Just because homophobic adults are uncomfortable with my sexual orientation doesn't mean I have to stay closeted around their children. I know I am not "recruiting" children or molesting them. The example of my loving can have a positive influence. Children who are lesbian/gay need open role models. Children who are bisexual need to know they have choices. Children who are heterosexual need to know that all love is beautiful.

There is much I can teach children by being open and honest about who I am and by being unafraid to show affection for my partner around them. I am a gift to the children I know, and I participate in their lives with pride.

November 30   **Sense of Community**

Since I've had AIDS I've seen so much to admire. We've developed so many support groups and buddy systems. For this much love, care, and compassion to come out of this community proves that we truly are people of incredible love. We're going to be a better community because of this.

Leonard Matlovich
quoted by Mike Hippler
Matlovich

December

December 1   **Sense of Community**

<u>I am creatively building a supportive community for myself.</u>

    I am ready for the support I want and deserve in fellowship with others. Even though it takes energy, the search for community is important to my well-being.

    With the growing number of groups for lesbians and gay men, I may be able to find churches, support or therapy groups, social or political organizations, clubs or bars for those of same-sex orientation. Activities in which lesbians and gay men participate also give me a sense of community—special concerts and festivals, plays and movies, lectures and workshops, Gay Pride and political-action events. Working on the campaigns of lesbian and gay political candidates can help me feel a part of a group. Even having a gay plumber or a lesbian veterinarian can help me feel less alone.

    In small towns and rural areas the challenge is greater. I may need to travel to more populated areas for my support. Reading gay newspapers, magazines and books, or listening to music by lesbian and gay performers, gives me some feeling of connection, but I also need personal contact whenever possible.

    Regardless of my method, I am reaching out to people who share my same-sex loving, and finding that I do have a sense of belonging. I am taking care of myself by connecting with others.

December 2   **Uniqueness**

*   It was okay to be gay, okay to be different. And being different didn't mean a life of loneliness and solitude. I learned that my friends and I could be different together. I was not merely out of the closet, I was out of the coffin.*

Aaron Fricke
quoted by Ann Heron
One Teenager in Ten

December 3   **Uniqueness**

<u>I celebrate all the aspects of the special person I am.</u>

    My uniqueness is part of my beauty, and I affirm my distinctness in defiance of a world that values sameness. I feel different because of my sexual orientation, but I am also different in other ways. I look at other aspects of who I am that separate me from what is dominant in my culture—race, religion, ancestry, age, gender, economic status, mental or physical differences. If I suffer discrimination because of more than one aspect of who I am, I have special challenges.

Part of my decision-making in life involves prioritizing where to spend my energy. Perhaps I need to assert myself more in one arena than another. Depending on my goals, I work toward establishing my rightful place in various contexts. While I don't have to fight all the battles of the universe, politically or personally, I know I am on this earth for a reason; I explore what that reason is.

In a society that undervalues me, I assert my full richness. That others don't always welcome my gifts makes no difference; I still offer them. That my culture wants me to conform doesn't matter; I continue to be who I am. That the mainstream resists my work to change it is irrelevant; I am transforming my surroundings day by day. Exalting my differences, I am confident of my worth in every unique aspect of who I am.

December 4 — Affirming Life

Looking back at my suicide attempt, I realize that this low point was really a turning point. Somewhere, pushed very deep down, the real reasons for continuing to live were already inside me. These reasons were, I think, that in my twisted, self-defeating way, I had a lot of pushed-down feelings of love to express that were struggling to get out. And that no matter how much of a failure I felt, I really did make some sort of difference in the world—with some people, somewhere.

Norma McCorvey
I Am Roe

December 5 — Affirming Life

<u>I affirm life by taking care of myself right now.</u>

My existence has meaning and importance. I remind myself of that reality when the struggles of life challenge me and I question whether I have the strength to continue living. Sexual orientation issues add to personal problems and give me much to deal with.

Today I look at what I need to do for myself right now. If I have suicidal feelings, I seek outside help. Even asking for help takes energy, but I gather my strength and reach out. There are people who care about me. I surround myself with them in my mind. I have the courage to contact at least one of them.

Although I may not be able to see my reasons for living at the moment, I know they are there. Others can help me get in touch with what is important for me. I go slowly in my decision-making, getting input from professionals, from friends or family, from my higher power. I put off making decisions until I feel centered.

I live my life one minute at a time. Even if it is impossible to see right now, I trust that my future can be better than the present.

Today I choose to go on. I move forward in dealing with the how and why of being alive, trusting that serenity and happiness lie before me.

December 6 — Journaling

I realized that our history needed to be told again and again, with many voices. I decided to come out of the closet as a writer. It was, in truth, a way to make up for my silence in the past.

Phyllis Burke
Family Values

December 7 — Journaling

I assert my value as a person through journaling. Forming the words that tell about me reminds me that I am lovable. When so many people prefer the comfort of my silence and invisibility, it is tempting to hide, even from myself. Sharing my story on paper through journaling is a way of asserting who I am. My writing can be private, but as I journal, I validate my reality. My words affirm that I am worth the energy of giving my thoughts and feelings some permanence. I write about crises and trivia, pain and joy, days and years. Exploring my mind and heart, writings clarify who I am. They help me remember or send a message to others, whether I deliver it or not. Bringing my inner truth to the light outside gives me peace on difficult issues I have faced.

Considering carefully what feels safe, I decide if I am ready to share what I write with others. Even if others reject what I write or choose not to read it, my act of offering it to them is the assertion of my value as a person. I am asking for the respect I deserve, and I am giving that respect to myself. My written words are weaving love for myself into a new decoration for my soul.

December 8 — Lesbian and Gay Equality

Outsiders mistakenly believe that gay communities or gay churches and temples are formed around sexual orientation. Rather, I believe that our communities and congregations are formed around our shared experience of adversity, suffering, and vulnerability in the face of pervasive homophobia and heterosexism. Our communities and churches and temples also celebrate our responses to our experience: our political achievements of liberation, our personal risks of identification with our people (even from within the closet), our vocational commitments to better our community, and our spiritual accomplishments of humble, compassionate service.

Chris Glaser
Coming Home

December 9   **Lesbian and Gay Equality**

<u>I am helping attain human rights for lesbians and gay men.</u>

I see progress in the struggle to secure human rights for lesbians and gay men. Sometimes there are backward steps, and always I am impatient for faster forward motion. The struggle takes so much energy from other parts of my life.
I let myself celebrate the progress that has been made, while envisioning what still needs to change. No matter what I do, I am having an impact. Even if I don't think of myself as a political activist, there are many levels at which I can act. My contribution is significant, whatever my choices.
Change can occur in subtle ways. Every time I come out to another person, or sign a petition, or talk about equality for lesbians and gay men, or call someone on a homophobic joke, I am acting on behalf of equal justice for all people. Giving myself credit for my part in the struggle, I commit myself to the work ahead. A better world is coming into being with my help.

December 10   **Relationship Building**

I intend to keep this glowing going, to do what's in my power so both of us stay happy. To hold on when we're not. To work at it till we get happy again. That's what I intend.

Jeanne Adleman
quoted by Marcy Adelman
Long Time Passing

December 11   **Relationship Building**

<u>I am willing to do my share to create successful relationships.</u>

Living in a relationship nourishes me, but a relationship also requires effort. As I struggle with conflict in a relationship, I acknowledge that all couples have problems. Society's hostility to my same-sex loving adds special obstacles, but there will always be differences to work out, in this relationship or any other.
I look at what I want from my relationship—love, intimacy, sex, fun, challenge, companionship, trust, respect, security, commitment, honest communication, financial sharing, emotional support—an awesome list. Am I expecting too much? I look at alternative ways of meeting needs that aren't being satisfied with my partner, while I continue to work on issues within the relationship. In all my interactions, I strive to be respectful of my commitment and the dignity of both of us.
With an open mind, I explore my part in the struggle. I'm not perfect, and I am willing to make changes, just as I would like my partner to change. Part of my resis-

tance is my fear of what I may have to give up for the relationship to improve. We cannot continue as a couple if either of us has to give up too much. Each of us needs to preserve a sense of personhood and integrity.

Seeking outside help can help us work through our issues, whether through a therapist, a support group, or discussion with friends and family. Exploring couple concerns with others by myself or with my partner, I find new perspectives. When I feel my resources are limited because of my same-sex orientation, I open myself to options, and guidance comes.

Today I recognize that building a successful relationship will take self-awareness, willingness to risk, and hard work on both our parts. I am ready to do my share—to give and receive, to learn and grow, to strive for a lasting love.

December 12 — Sexuality

Allowed the freedom to be human, we might find that a new sexuality would emerge, encompassing not only the sensual, but also the trans-physical qualities of love, empathy and concern for one another's personhood, regardless of gender.

Del Martin and Phyllis Lyon
Lesbian/Woman

December 13 — Sexuality

I claim the validity of my sexuality.

I was created to be a sexual person, and I explore what that means for me. I take no heed of those who contend that sex with my same-sex partner is perverted because I can't reproduce through it. If it were, then sex with post-menopausal or infertile heterosexuals should also be considered deviant. I know that is not true. There are many reasons to be sexual, and I consider the validity of each for me.

Sexual contact is pleasureful. I enjoy the touch I get and find satisfaction in giving pleasure to my partner. Feeling good is not evil.

Sexual communication is part of how I express myself. Deep within me is a longing for intimacy with myself and others. Intimacy happens on many levels, and sexual intimacy is an important aspect. Through my lovemaking, I find connection, I nurture and am nurtured, I open myself to another person as well as to my own self-knowledge. It is a communion of my whole self.

I am participating in the rhythm of the universe when I am being sexual. My lovemaking creates new bonds as well as new life within myself and my sexual partner, even though it doesn't create a baby.

I decide what sex means to me and act accordingly. I am a joyful sexual being, with reasons that are right for me.

December 14   **Expecting Basic Rights**

I don't think that harassment and using threatening language is freedom of speech. If you can't shout fire in a crowded theatre, why should you be able to shout faggot in a homophobic society?

Gary Schiff
Equal Time

December 15   **Expecting Basic Rights**

<u>I deserve respect and fair treatment, regardless of others' attitudes.</u>

I need people in my life who give me more than tolerance, but I neither expect nor ask for wholehearted approval from everyone. In my same-sex orientation, I know many people will continue to disapprove of me, just as I don't approve of all the people I know. As a human being, though, I deserve to be treated with respect, even by people who condemn my sexual orientation. If this country stands for freedom and equality, then discrimination against me and my sisters and brothers must end.

I work for fair treatment, while recognizing other people's rights to their own attitudes. I support reasonable laws, but I know the laws cannot change feelings, they can only require or prohibit specific actions.

I proudly assert my right to basic human dignity. With strength and courage, I pursue my vision in a reluctant world; I fight for the freedom to be open about who I am, without fear of persecution.

December 16   **Inventing a Celebration**

The rules break like a thermometer,
quicksilver spills across the charted systems,
we're out in a country that has no language
no laws, we're chasing the raven and the wren
through gorges unexplored since dawn
whatever we do together is pure invention
the maps they gave us were out of date
by years...

Adrienne Rich
"Twenty-One Love Poems: XIII"
The Fact of a Doorframe

December 17 **Inventing a Celebration**

I pay attention to what I need for myself during the holidays.
    Defining holidays as a time of festivity, I explore what I need to be joyful. Often this time of year is filled with extra "shoulds" for me. I "should" spend the holidays with my family of origin; I "should" be thankful for everything I have; I "should" party and be happy.
    In my same-sex orientation I feel even more stress: decisions about partner involvement in celebrations, the ever-present coming-out issues, sensitive topics of conversation to avoid or confront. Sometimes I wish the holidays would just go away!
    I face the fact that I can choose whether or not to celebrate the holidays. One real option is to ignore them—they *will* go away with time! I let myself know that I don't need to follow anyone's "shoulds," even the hardest ones to ignore—the ones I tell myself.
    Taking time out from the bustle, I ask myself what I really need this holiday season. That is the best holiday gift of all, and I deserve it. I celebrate ME this year!

December 18 **Sharing My Story**

To be mutually empathic and empowering is to learn not only how to listen and hear, well and deeply, but also how to speak honestly of ourselves and be heard from the depths of who we are.

Carter Heyward
Touching Our Strength

December 19 **Sharing My Story**

I share my pride in telling my story.
    Coming-out stories are a universal source of fascination.
    "When did you know you were gay?"
    "Who did you tell first?"
    "How did your parents react?"
    Straight or gay, casual acquaintances or longtime friends, even talk show audiences—they all seem curious.
    My coming-out story is at the core of who I am. I open myself to others as I share that knowledge, and I draw close to others as I hear their stories. When revealing myself to straight people feels too threatening, I seek other same-sex oriented people. If I don't know lesbians or gay men who live near me, I can contact people in other areas. Travel-

ing to places where there are groups of lesbians and gay men creates new options for me.
   Gathering my courage to talk about who I am, I sense the strength growing inside me. When people listen, I feel valued. When I share, I affirm myself.
   My story is important, and I want to hear what others have experienced. As I open myself to connections with people, I am validating the beautiful message of my loving.

December 20 — Winter Celebration

I want a holiday celebration like [the Seder celebration at Passover] for us gays, and I plan to stage one. It will have a meal with various foods being symbolic of the experiences of our gay ancestors. We will mourn our dead and pay tribute to their endurance. We will thank them for having made it possible for us to be here today in greater freedom than most of them experienced. I would like to blend into the ceremony some of the printed words of gay poets and writers, past and present. I would like to have a place in the ceremony where each person at the table can offer some personal thanks.

Don Clark
Living Gay

December 21 — Winter Celebration
Winter Solstice

<u>I fashion a holiday season of my own choosing.</u>

   This is the time for people of many traditions to celebrate—Hanukkah, Feast of Lights and Feast of Dedication in the Jewish faith; Winter Solstice for those of pagan beliefs; Christmas for Christians celebrating the birth of Jesus; Kwanzaa, an African-American cultural holiday. I consider what my celebration is to be. If I am not comfortable with the tradition I was raised in, I can choose my own festivities, whether adopted or created. Seeing the holidays commercialized and exploited can make me question whether their simplicity and meaning are lost. In my same-sex loving that seems so far outside my established heritage, the entire process may feel designed for someone else.
   This culture cannot steal my right to a special jubilee. I reach deeply into my wisdom and see that I have something to celebrate. Gently I bring it forth, holding it carefully, presenting my festival offering to myself. I can fashion the holiday of my choosing this season if I so desire. I give my energy to whatever observance I value, whether it is traditional or newly invented, and in so doing, I honor myself.

December 22 **Winter Celebration**
Winter Solstice

Here is how I design my own celebration of the winter holidays: _____

_____

_____

_____

_____

December 23 **Playfulness**

Today we can decide to live like the kind of grown-up person who hops on merry-go-rounds, picks daisies, and dances. We can lay in the grass and watch ants work. We can choose to live today with no regrets about the past. After all, our past brought us to this marvelous place, this moment of creation, this totally new day.

Perry Tilleraas
The Color of Light

December 24 **Playfulness**

<u>I bring my inner child out into the light.</u>

There is a merry child within me, ready for playtime and fun. In my child times, when it would have been normal to be especially frolicsome, I may have been serious because of coming to grips with being different. As an adult, I still need the playful side of myself. Responsibility and whimsy can go hand in hand.

Today I look within for my fanciful self. I may have to search deeply. There are different kinds of closets. My child may be hiding in one.

I give that child permission to come into the light, to be uninhibited, to laugh and be silly and find joy. Embracing a fresh perspective, I put sadness and hurt aside for awhile. A new being emerges, running barefoot, seeing the world through wide eyes, with wonder and excitement and a giggle!

December 25 **Giving**

As sober, proud, and responsible gay men and lesbians who touch other people's lives with the richness of our diversity today and every day, we continue our journey together. Wishing everyone the joy of the journey, I hope we may all meet along the way to celebrate our gifts and the gift-givers.

Sheppard Kominars
Accepting Ourselves

December 26   Giving

<u>I am a gift-giver to the universe.</u>
    Holidays and giving don't have to be equated with commercialism. Thinking about the tradition of offering presents, I reflect on giving the intangible. I give a gift of myself to those I love whenever I share my time, my energy, my thoughts, my feelings. When granted without reservation, these gifts are truly priceless.
    In my same-sex orientation, I deal with a world that often discounts what I have to offer. Today I affirm the special talents and wisdom I bring to the benefit of all around me. Moving beyond the desire for acknowledgment of my gifts, I go about my living without apology. My reward is the satisfaction of being able to contribute. I offer the gift that is me to the universe.

December 27   Hopes

> *"Hope" is the thing with feathers -*
> *That perches in the soul -*
> *And sings the tune without the words -*
> *And never stops - at all -*
>
> *And sweetest - in the Gale - is heard -*
> *And sore must be the storm -*
> *That could abash the little Bird*
> *That kept so many warm -*
>
> *I've heard it in the chillest land -*
> *And on the strangest Sea -*
> *Yet, never, in Eternity,*
> *It asked a crumb - of me.*
>
> Emily Dickinson

December 28   Hopes

<u>I move beyond the holidays with my hopes for future holiday seasons.</u>
    As I congratulate myself on concluding another holiday season in my life, I may feel like the child who has opened all the presents and says, "Is that all?" With the anticipation beforehand, the glitter of decorations, the plans for special times with loved ones, the holidays rarely measure up to my expectations. Issues related to my same-sex orientation have the potential for added disappointment. I won't make myself feel worse by thinking I shouldn't feel the way I do. If I am sad, my sadness is understandable. I don't have to feel happy just because of the holiday season. I recall parts of the holiday season that did feel good, and enjoy my memories of those experiences.

As I look back over what has happened, I acknowledge that I did my best, and I did well. Looking ahead, I consider whether I want to plan differently next year. To assure that I won't forget, I can put my thoughts in writing. Perhaps I need to devise some way of achieving closure on some interactions with others. Or I may be ready to let it all go without further thought.

Although some of my hopes weren't met, I still look forward to the future, confident in the knowledge that I can make the best of all situations. I am wiser, I am stronger, and I nurture my new vision for holiday seasons to come.

December 29 — Diversity

We know we do not have to become copies of each other in order to be able to work together. We know that when we join hands across the table of our difference, diversity gives us power. When we can arm ourselves with the strength and vision from our diverse communities, then we will in truth, all of us—be free at last!

Audre Lorde
1983 Civil Rights March
Washington, D.C.

December 30 — Diversity

<u>I celebrate my place in the rainbow of humanity.</u>

Embracing the rainbow as a symbol of lesbian and gay pride, I appreciate the beauty of distinctly different colors blending to form a spectacular wonder of nature.

When I am pressured to be someone different from who I really am, I remind myself that the rainbow would lose its majesty if it were only one color. And which color is best? None! Each is striking alone, and yet glorious in complementing the rest of the heavenly arch.

Today I rejoice in the way I complement the human family, for I know I am an important part of the diversity of nature. With pride, I claim my identity as a special person, shining forth with distinctness, bringing variety to the rainbow of humanity.

December 31 — Unity of Time
New Year's Eve

They say we do not occupy a part of time, that each of our lives is a consciousness which extends through the whole of time. Each of our consciousnesses is a way of knowing, a knowledge, a conception, of the whole of time. Therefore there are many times, not one.

River Malcolm
"The Women Talk About How They Live"
Sinister Wisdom

I affirm my rootedness in the whole of time.

As I begin a new year, I place my life in the context of time. My moments are a blend of what was, is and shall be. In one sense, I only have the present. Yet, what is now came out of what was, and leads into what will be. I draw on the timelessness of yesterday, today and tomorrow.

The challenges in my same-sex loving may tempt me to deny the pain of the past or the insecurity of the future, but all of it is mine to claim. I take possession of my whole life today.

I look forward to adventures in my future and hold the lessons of the past in my heart, but I live fully each moment of my present. I am thankful to be alive and consider carefully the choices I have for spending my time.

We celebrate the beginning of the year by taking on a new number, but in truth it is simply the continuation of seconds, minutes, hours, days, weeks, and months that have been passing through the ages. I celebrate my place in time, and embrace the present in motion.

Eleanor Ruth Wagner 137

Subject Index

Age: Mar 17, 18; Jul 7, 8
AIDS/HIV: Feb 19, 20; Mar 13, 14; May 30; Jul 31; Aug 1; Oct 6, 7; Nov 30
Anger: Feb 9, 10; Apr 12, 13; Jul 11,12; Oct 27, 28
Aspirations: Jan 14, 15; Mar 19; May 20, 21; Jun 4, 5, 10, 11; Nov 11; Dec 28
Body Image: Sep 26, 27; Nov 18
Boundaries: Sep 10, 15, 16; Nov 19
Breaking Up: Feb 25, 26; Aug 16, 30, 31; Oct 17, 18; Nov 15
Celebrations: Feb 13, 14; May 26, 27; Aug 6, 7; Oct 12; Nov 24, 25; Dec 16, 17, 20, 21, 22, 26
Change: Jan 18, 19; Feb 18, 21, 22; Mar 21; Oct 2, 3; Nov 14, 15
Chemical Dependency: Apr 30; May 1
Children: May 16, 17; Jun 24, 25; Nov 28, 29
Coming Out: Jan 2, 3; Feb 2, 7, 8; Mar 1, 2, 20; Apr 4, 5, 19; Jun 12, 13; Jul 19, 20, 26; Aug 8, 9, 22, 23; Sep 11, 17, 18, Oct 10, 11; Dec 2, 19
Community: Jul 13, 14; Mar 5, 6; May 15; Jun 20, 21; Aug 2, 3; Sep 24, 25; Nov 1, 2, 19; Dec 1, 8, 19, 29
Depression: Jan 29; Feb 18; Apr 2, 3; Aug 24, 25; Nov 7, 8; Dec 4, 5, 28
Diversity: Jan 20, 21; Dec 29, 30
Family: Feb 15, 16; Jun 8, 9; Sep 30; Oct 1; Nov 16
Friendship: Jan 4, 5; Mar 3, 4; Jul 17, 18; Aug 10, 17; Sep 9
Gender: Nov 9, 10
Happiness: Mar 22, 23; Apr 18; Oct 19; Nov 22, 23
Healing: Feb 20; May 12, 13; Jun 18, 19

Healing from Abuse: Mar 7, 8; Jul 21, 22; Oct 15, 16
Homophobia: Apr 8, 9; Jun 2, 3; Aug 26, 27; Nov 13, 17; Dec 14, 15
Inner Strength: Mar 24, 25; Sep 13, 14, 22, 23; Dec 18, 27
Journaling: Dec 6, 7
Minority Status: May 8, 9; Jun 16, 17; Sep 28, 29; Dec 2, 3
Nature's Power: Jan 6, 7; Apr 22, 23; May 29; Sep 21
Passion: Oct 8, 9
Patience: Oct 21, 22
Personal Safety: Feb 8, 10; Mar 31; May 24, 25; Jun 28, 29
Playfulness: Apr 1; May 4, 5; Dec 23, 24
Political Choices: Jan 26, 27; Jun 30; Jul 2, 4, 29, 30; Aug 14, 15; Nov 2, 20, 21; Dec 9, 15
Pride: Jan 9, 10, 11; Feb 27, 28; Jun 26, 27; Jul 15; Aug 18, 19; Dec 19
Quest for Guidance: Nov 5, 6
Relationship with Self: Jan 8, 28; Feb 1, 5, 6; Mar 11; Jul 5, 6; Aug 4, 5, 20, 21; Sep 3, 4; Oct 19, 20, 23; Nov 12
Relationship with a Lover: Jan 12, 13; Feb 3, 4; Mar 9, 10, 28, 29; Apr 6, 7, 20, 26, 27; May 6, 7, 28; Jun 14, 15; Jul 27, 28; Oct 29, 30; Nov 12; Dec 10, 11
Religion/Spirituality: Jan 30, 31; Feb 11, 12; Apr 10, 11; May 10, 11, 22, 23, 31; Jun 22; Oct 24, 31; Nov 6; Dec 31
Respect: Apr 21; Jun 1; Jul 3; Sep 10; Oct 22; Nov 16, 17
Seeking Help: Nov 8; Dec 5
Self-Esteem: Jan 1, 24, 25; Feb 23, 24, 16, 17; Apr 16, 17; May 2, 3; Jul 9, 10, 25, 26; Aug 11, 17; Nov 12
Sex: Aug 12, 13; Sep 1, 2; Oct 25, 26
Sexuality: Jan 22, 23; Mar 15, 16; Apr 24, 25, 28, 29; Oct 4, 5; Dec 12, 13
Sexual Orientation: Jan 16, 17; Mar 12, 26, 27; Apr 14, 15; Jun 6, 7; Jul 23, 24; Aug 28, 29
Taking Risks: Mar 30; May 14; Jun 14, 15; Sep 7, 8, 11, 19, 20; Oct 13, 14; Dec 18
Times of Inactivity: Nov 26, 27
Wholeness: May 18, 19; Jun 23; Jul 1, 16; Sep 5, 6, 12, 22; Dec 3, 31
Youth: Nov 3, 4; Dec 2

Author

Eleanor Ruth Wagner lives in Minneapolis, MN with her partner, Kathy. An audiologist and mother of two adult sons, Ms. Wagner holds a Bachelor of Arts degree from the College of Wooster, and a Master of Arts degree from the University of Illinois. In addition to writing affirmations, she conducts affirmational workshops for lesbians.

(Photo Peterson Portraits)

Photographer

Born in Italy, raised in Sweden, Victor Arimondi is an internationally recognized photographer and model. Exhibitions of his photographs have been mounted in San Francisco, Tokyo, Copenhagen and New York. In 1994, the Stockholm Museum of Modern Art presented a retrospective of his work.

Related books available from Alamo Square:

Being • Being Happy • Being Gay
Bert Herrman

Pathways to a Rewarding Life for Lesbians and Gay Men. The gay make-your-life-work book. "Herrman extends a compassionate and useful hand in the journey toward realizing our full human potential." —Mark Thompson, *The Advocate*.

Alamo Square Press   ISBN: 0-9624751-0-6   128 pages/paper/$8.00

In God's Image
Fr. Robert Warren Cromey(Episc.)

Christian Witness to the Need for Gay/Lesbian Equality in the Eyes of the Church. "Nurturing, healing...a call to action."—Malcolm Boyd.

Alamo Square Press   ISBN: 0-9624751-2-2   128 pages/paper/$9.95

Out of the Bishop's Closet
Antonio A. Feliz

The Daring Testimony of Faith of a Gay Mormon High Priest. Fleeing the terror of the Church, Feliz escapes with secrets that would make Brigham Young turn pale.

Alamo Square Press   ISBN: 0-9624751-7-3   208 pages/paper/$12.95

What the Bible Really Says About Homosexuality
Daniel A. Helminiak, Ph.D.

Recent findings by top scholars offer a radical new view. The long-awaited, mind-expanding bestseller by a Roman Catholic Priest and respected theologian.

Alamo Square Press   ISBN: 0-9624751-9-X   128 pages/paper/$9.95

The Lord is My Shepherd & He Knows I'm Gay
Rev. Troy Perry

The courageous life story of the founder of the Metropolitan Community Church, the largest gay/lesbian Christian denomination and one of the fastest-growing Christian denominations in the country. 25th Anniversary Edition.

UFMCC   ISBN: 1-885591-45-4   264 pages/paper/$10.95

Holy Homosexuals
Rev. Michael S. Piazza

The truth about being gay or lesbian and Christian by the senior pastor of the world's largest gay and lesbian church.

Sources of Hope   ISBN: 1-887129-00-6   208 pages/paper/$11.98

Sex With God
Thomas O'Neil

Torn between forbidden gay love and love for God, a poet shouts to heaven. "Splendid! Beautiful!"—*New York Native.*

Wexford Press   ISBN: 0-9622398-1-X   176 pages/paper/$6.95

Sex and Spirit
Robert Barzan, Editor

Exploring Gay Men's Spirituality. Essays by gay writers on the wide diversity of paths and visions of gay men. "Any gay man who has ever pondered about sex or wondered how being gay fits into the grand scheme of things, should not be without this book."—*Bay Area Reporter.*

White Crane Press   ISBN: 0-9645384-0-7   144 pages/paper/$10.95

Those People at That Church Cookbook

The Lutheran Church that was thrown out of the Synod for ordaining gay and lesbian ministers has published a fabulous cookbook with stirring sidenotes by community members who share the joys of being in an "open" church.

St. Francis Lutheran Church   ISBN: 09642337-1-1   256 pages/paper/$18.95

For your copies, send a check or money order for total cost of books desired, plus a shipping fee of $2.00 for the first book and $.50 for each additional book to:

Alamo Square Press
P.O. Box 14543
San Francisco, CA 94114

306.76
WAG
AUTHOR   Wagner, Eleanor Ruth

TITLE   Lavender Reflections

DATE LOANED	BORROWER'S NAME	DATE RETURNED

306.76
WAG

Wagner, Eleanor Ruth

Lavender Reflections

FRANCISCAN CENTER
1784 LaCrosse Avenue
St. Paul, MN 55119